SAFE OPERATION OF FIRE TANKERS

FEMA

U.S. Fire Administration

U.S. Fire Administration
Mission Statement

As an entity of the Federal Emergency Management Agency, the mission of the United States Fire Administration is to reduce life and economic losses due to fire and related emergencies, through leadership, advocacy, coordination, and support. We serve the National Independently, in coordination with other Federal agencies, and in partnership with fire protection and emergency service communities. With a commitment to excellence, we provide public education, training, technology, and data initiatives.

TABLE OF CONTENTS

INTRODUCTION

One needs to look no further than the name of our profession, the *fire service*, in order to gain a keen insight into some of its most basic tenets. First is the notion that the primary mission of our profession always has been to protect the public against the ravages of fire. Obviously, in recent years that role has been expanded to include the delivery of a multitude of other emergency services, including emergency medical services, nonfire rescue services, hazardous materials incident mitigation, and others. Even though today's fire departments respond to more of these nonfire events than they do fires, the word *fire* still remains our "middle name" in most cases (for example, the Anytown *Fire* Department).

Just as important as the word *fire* is the word *service* when examining our mission. Our most basic mission is to *deliver* a vital service to our customers or constituents. When they have a fire, become ill, or are entrapped, we respond to mitigate the situation as much as possible. The key principle here is that we must respond to the constituent's location. Rarely do they bring the problem to us.

Because we understand the urgency of their need, it is our goal to respond to their location as expeditiously as possible. To that end, emergency responders are given many liberties that are not afforded other members of the driving public. Emergency vehicles are equipped with warning devices that signal other drivers to clear the way. Emergency vehicles are given the option of continuing through intersections when other vehicles must heed a signal to stop. In some cases, emergency vehicles are even allowed to travel against the normal flow of traffic or at speeds above the posted limits.

Each of these liberties, along with a myriad other factors that will be detailed later in this report, increases the amount of risk imposed upon firefighters and the apparatus in which they ride. In fact, apparatus crashes that occur when responding to or returning from emergency incidents are historically the second leading cause of firefighter deaths in the United States. Each year approximately 25 percent of all firefighters deaths are attributed to apparatus crashes.

When reviewing the statistics regarding fire apparatus crashes, it becomes very apparent that a disproportionately high number of these crashes involve fire department tanker apparatus. The reasons for the disproportionate number of crashes involving fire department tankers will be detailed in the main body of this report.

For the purpose of this report, the term **tanker** is used to describe ground vehicles that are used to supply firefighting water to rural and suburban locations not equipped with a fixed water supply system. In jurisdictions that use the Incident Command System, these types of vehicles are referred to as tenders or water tenders. The generic term applied to these vehicles by the National Fire Protection Association (NFPA) is "mobile water supply apparatus."

To meet the definition of a mobile water supply apparatus according to the NFPA Standard 1901, *Standard for Automotive Fire Apparatus*, a vehicle must carry a minimum of 1,000 gallons of water. The most common water capacities of tankers in the United States range from 1,500 to 3,000 gallons. However, capacities of up to 5,000 gallons on a straight chassis and 10,000 gallons on a tractor-trailer apparatus are not unheard of.

The alarming rate at which fire department tankers are involved in serious crashes led the United States Fire Administration (USFA) to commission this report. Since its inception, the USFA has been committed to enhancing the health and safety of emergency response personnel. Fire service personnel across the United States rely on the USFA for current information and state-of-the-art guidance on critical fire service operational issues. The purposes of this report include:

- documenting all fatal crashes involving fire department tankers since 1990;

- analyzing the causes and common factors associated with these crashes;

- highlighting pertinent case histories that show examples of the problem;

- providing information on reducing the frequency of these crashes and minimizing their severity/impact when unavoidable crashes occur; and

- providing example procedures and checklists to assist departments in reducing the likelihood of tanker crashes.

The USFA enlisted the help of several groups of fire service professionals in order to develop this report. The effort was led and coordinated by IOCAD Emergency Services Group. Providing invaluable assistance to this effort was the staff of Volunteer Fireman's Insurance Services (VFIS). VFIS has long been a leader in the area of safe fire apparatus operation and training. The group of subject-matter-experts and other Federal agencies listed below also provided information, feedback, and encouragement that led to this final product:

Gene P. Carlson, Volunteer Fireman's Insurance Services (VFIS)

Jeffrey M. Dickey, National Association of Emergency Vehicle Technicians

Stephen N. Foley, National Fire Protection Association (NFPA)

Paul S. Lukas, National Volunteer Fire Council (NVFC)

Glenn McCallister, Semo Tanks, Rep. Fire Apparatus Manufacturer's Association (FAMA)

Robert Murgallis, FEMA/United States Fire Administration (USFA)

Eric D. Nagle, IOCAD Emergency Services

Kevin M. Roche, Phoenix Fire Department (Principal Project Researcher)

Bill Troup, FEMA/United States Fire Administration (USFA)

Michael A. Wieder, Oklahoma State University, Fire Protection Publications (IFSTA) (Principal Project Writer)

Michael Wilbur, Emergency Vehicle Response/Firehouse Magazine

Fred C. Windisch, IAFC, Volunteer & Combination Chief Officers Section

Michael L. Young, Volunteer Firemen's Insurance Services (VFIS)

The USFA would also like to acknowledge and thank the following agencies and individuals who assisted by providing photographs, illustrations, and information used to complete this report:

Edmond, Oklahoma, Fire Department

IFSTA/Fire Protection Publications, Oklahoma State University

Ron Jeffers, Union City, New Jersey

Ron Bogardus, Albany, New York

Volunteer Firemen's Insurance Services (VFIS), York, Pennsylvania

Bob Barraclough, Plano, Texas

Joel Woods, Maryland Fire & Rescue Institute (MFRI)

National Institute for Occupational Safety and Health (NIOSH)

National Fallen Firefighters Foundation

Firehouse Magazine

It is hoped that fire department leaders and training officials will use the information contained in this document to reduce the risk of their fire department tankers becoming involved in some type of a crash. Some of the information in this document pertains to apparatus design issues. Other information pertains to driver training and standard operating procedural issues. All of the information, when analyzed and implemented appropriately, can lessen the frequency and severity of crashes involving fire department tankers.

CAUSES OF FIRE DEPARTMENT TANKER CRASHES

In order to implement a program to reduce the frequency and severity of crashes involving fire department tankers, it is necessary to review and understand the factors that have influenced such incidents in the past. When reviewing the various reports and case histories of tanker crashes that have occurred in the past 10 years or so, numerous common factors or trends begin to emerge. With this information in hand, fire department officers and training personnel are able to effectively develop standard operating procedures, policies, and training programs that address this issue.

The purpose of this chapter, as well as the chapter that follows, is to highlight the factors that research has proved play a significant role in tanker crashes. The remainder of this document will then be focused on strategies for reducing and minimizing these incidents in the future.

In their manual titled, *Pumping Apparatus Driver/Operator Handbook*, the International Fire Service Training Association (IFSTA) suggests that the causes of all fire apparatus crashes can be grouped into one of five categories:

1. *Improper backing of the apparatus* -- Backing crashes are among the most frequent of all types of fire apparatus crashes. While they are seldom serious in terms of injury or death, they do account for a significant portion of overall damage costs **(Figure 1-1)**.

2. *Reckless driving by the public* -- This category includes a variety of reckless actions, including failure to obey traffic signals, excessive speed, failure to yield to emergency vehicles, and other common civilian driving behaviors.

3. *Excessive speed by the fire apparatus driver* -- Excessive speed may result in the driver losing control of the vehicle or being unable to stop the vehicle before hitting another vehicle or object.

4. *Lack of driving skill and experience by the fire apparatus driver* -- This may be due to insufficient training of the driver or unfamiliarity with the exact vehicle being driven.

5. *Poor apparatus design or maintenance* -- While this can be the case with custom-built fire apparatus, it is a more significant problem in departments that use retrofitted or home-built apparatus.

Figure 1-1 Backing crashes are among the most common types of fire apparatus crashes. *Courtesy of Ron Jeffers*

These five categories account for the vast majority of all crashes involving fire department tankers. In reality, there are a number of subfactors within each of these categories that are worthy of exploration. In this chapter, we will explore each of these subfactors in depth. This report loosely categorizes these causal factors into five broad classifications:

1. Human Factors
2. Apparatus Design Factors
3. Driving Surface Factors
4. Emergency Scene Factors
5. Other Factors

HUMAN FACTORS

A significant portion, if not the majority, of causes of fire department tanker crashes can be traced to at least one human factor. Depending on the situation this error in judgment may be attributed to the driver of the tanker, the driver of another fire department vehicle, or a civilian motorist. Of all the factors that we will review in this document, human factors are the most difficult to correct and control. Apparatus and roads can be designed and maintained properly, and emergency scenes can be managed in an orderly fashion. However, it is much harder to control the actions of humans on a consistent basis. This section looks at the more common human factors associated with fire department tanker crashes.

Insufficient Training

Perhaps the most unfortunate human factor associated with fire department tanker crashes is a driver who has not been appropriately trained to drive that type of apparatus. National Fire Protection Association (NFPA) Standard 1500, *Standard on Fire Department Occupational Health and Safety Program* (2002 edition), clearly states in requirement 5.1.2 that "*The fire department shall provide training and education for all fire department members commensurate with the duties and functions that they are expected to perform. Members shall be provided with training and education appropriate for their duties and responsibilities before being permitted to engage in emergency operations.*" Requirement 5.1.1 of that same standard requires the fire department to provide training that assures their members will carry out their assigned duties in a safe manner. Finally, requirement 5.2.2 of the standard requires all fire apparatus drivers to meet the applicable chapters of NFPA 1002, *Standard for Fire Apparatus Driver/Operator Professional Qualifications*, for the type of apparatus they are expected to drive.

All drivers must complete a thorough training program before being allowed to drive a fire department tanker under nonemergency or emergency conditions. The training needed prior to driving the apparatus on a public roadway includes a combination of classroom and practical instruction. The student driver should demonstrate the ability to operate the tanker safely on a controlled driving course before being allowed to begin test drives on unrestricted public roadways **(Figure 1-2)**.

Figure 1-2 Initial practical training should be conducted on a closed course, not a public roadway.

They also should demonstrate knowledge of the use of all of the various controls and equipment that are a part of the apparatus. Only after successfully completing all of this training should the driver be permitted to drive the tanker outside of training.

Departments also must resist the temptation to allow drivers who have been trained on other types of apparatus to automatically be allowed to drive tankers. The other types of apparatus (pumpers, rescue vehicles, brush apparatus, etc.) that the driver may have been trained on are considerably smaller and lighter than a fire department tanker. Those other apparatus may not be prone to the extreme operational considerations posed by tankers, including dramatic load/weight shifts, high centers of gravity, and increased stopping distances as a result of their heavy weight. They may also be unaware of simple tanker characteristics such as the fact that the apparatus is lighter and will travel faster when the water tank is empty, which makes the vehicle more likely to skid under certain conditions. If a previously trained driver is going to be expected to drive a fire department tanker, the driver must receive additional training on the tanker before being allowed to operate that vehicle.

Detailed information on designing appropriate training programs for drivers of fire department tankers can be found in Chapter 4 of this document.

Insufficient Driver Experience

Many tanker crash investigations note that the driver involved in the crash had a limited amount of experience driving that vehicle. In reality, there is no way of avoiding putting new drivers behind the wheel of a tanker at some point in time. Everyone must have a starting point in his or her career. Hopefully, ensuring that drivers complete a thorough training program prior to being allowed to operate the vehicle under response conditions can minimize the dangers associated with limited experience. The training program should emphasize the fact that even though the drivers may complete the program and be certified to drive under emergency response conditions, they need to be extra cautious until they have a reasonable amount of experience to back up their training.

Overconfidence in Driving Ability

The goal of any training program is to motivate students to feel confident in their abilities once they are turned loose into the real world. However, the training program should be geared toward tempering the students' natural tendency to feel overconfident in their abilities when they are placed in real-life conditions. The driver's inflated sense of his or her own abilities can be especially problematic during the adrenaline rush of an emergency response. This may lead them to drive too fast or attempt maneuvers that they are not yet capable of safely completing, leading to a crash.

Another factor that can lead to overconfidence is the driver's perception that, because he or she has a clean, crash-free driving record to this point in his or her life, he or she will automatically be a good driver of the fire apparatus. Training of new drivers must reinforce the significant difference between driving a passenger vehicle versus driving a 15- to 30-ton fire department tanker.

Excessive Speed

In reviewing the records and reports on fire department tanker crashes that have occurred over the years, a large percentage of these reports list excessive speed of the apparatus as one of the primary contributing factors to the cause of the crash. There exists an old adage that "speed kills." This certainly seems to be the case when applied to fire apparatus crashes, in particular those involving tankers. The problems associated with excessive speed manifest themselves in a number of ways:

1. The vehicle is unable to negotiate a curve in the road.

2. The vehicle is unable to stop before hitting another vehicle or object.

3. The vehicle is unable to stop before entering an intersection or railroad crossing.

4. A weight shift occurs when the vehicle is slowed, causing it to skid or overturn.

5. Control of the vehicle is lost after hitting a pothole, speed bump, or similar defect in the driving surface.

6. Control of the vehicle is lost as a result of swaying outside the lane of travel and striking a median or curb, or the tires on one side of the vehicle (usually the right side) leave the road surface.

7. Tire traction is lost on wet, icy, snowy, or unpaved road surfaces.

Fire departments must develop and enforce policies that establish maximum speed criteria for all types of apparatus, including tankers. Drivers must be familiar with these policies and also understand that they are maximums. The policy should contain a provision that allows a riding company officer or superior to demand that the driver slow down, but never give them the right to force the driver to go faster than the driver's comfort level allows. Detailed information on driving at appropriate speeds is covered in Chapter 4 of this manual.

Inability to Recognize Danger Signs

A lack of training and/or experience on the part of the driver may result in an inability to recognize obvious signs of possible or impending danger in sufficient time to avoid the hazard. Training programs should emphasize looking ahead while driving and anticipating hazardous situations so that they may be avoided. This includes situations such as traversing busy intersections, anticipating ice on elevated road surfaces during borderline freezing conditions, and approaching curves that will require slowing the apparatus to negotiate them safely (**Figure 1-3**).

As reported in the IFSTA *Pumping Apparatus Driver/Operator Handbook,* a study conducted by the Society of Automotive Engineers (SAE) determined that in 42 percent of all crashes involving commercial truck drivers, the driver was not aware of a problem until it was too late to correct it. This finding would most likely be mirrored if a similar study had been

Figure 1-3 Drivers must be able to anticipate the hazards posed by a severe curve long before the apparatus enters the curve.

undertaken involving fire apparatus drivers. The principles of fire prevention and crash prevention are the same: it is much more effective to recognize and correct the hazards before they occur than it is to deal with them after it is too late.

Failure to Have or Follow Departmental SOP's

This category actually describes two different scenarios. The first covers those departments that have failed to formalize and implement standard operating procedures (SOP's) pertinent to the operation of fire department vehicles. This is most common in small, volunteer fire departments. However, crash investigations involving larger fire departments also have uncovered this reality. In these cases, any direction that had been provided to apparatus drivers was in the form of on-the-job training or word of mouth. Lacking any formal training or policies to follow, the tanker driver operates the vehicle in an unsafe manner and becomes involved in a crash.

The second scenario involves appropriately trained fire apparatus drivers failing to follow established departmental policies and SOP's. These SOP's must be enforced on a regular, consistent basis in order for them to be effective. Failure to follow SOP's should result in repercussions for the driver, whether or not they result in a crash.

One of the most common types of crashes that can be traced to failure to follow SOP's are those that involve backing the apparatus. In fact, backing crashes are among the most common of all types of fire apparatus crashes. While they rarely result in injury or death (though they have from time to time), they account for a significantly high portion of fire department insurance claims and damage repair costs. Most departments have established policies for apparatus backing maneuvers, including using safety guides equipped with

Figure 1-4 At least one and preferably two guides should be used anytime the apparatus needs to be backed up.

portable radios **(Figure 1-4)**. However, in the haste to move a vehicle on the emergency scene or in the security of simply backing the apparatus into the fire station, oftentimes the driver will attempt the maneuver without getting appropriate help. The end result is often backing the apparatus into another vehicle, a stationary object, or even a person. In virtually every case, the crash would have been avoided if the SOP's had simply been followed.

Disobeying Applicable Traffic Laws and Posted Regulations

Because of the perceived urgency during an emergency response, tanker drivers sometimes disobey traffic laws, including posted regulations. These include actions and consequences such as:

Figure 1-5 Fire apparatus drivers should always follow the posted speed limit or departmental policies on appropriate speed.

- *Exceeding the speed limit* -- This may result in losing control of the vehicle or the inability to stop before hitting another vehicle or object **(Figure 1-5)**.

- *Continuing through intersections against a red light or other stop signal* -- Failure to ensure that all lanes of traffic have yielded to the emergency vehicle may result in another vehicle entering the intersection at the same time and colliding with the fire apparatus.

- *Crossing the centerline of the road* -- This may be done when passing slowed or stopped vehicles. It is also commonly performed at intersections where stopped vehicles are blocking all lanes in the apparatus' direction of travel. Failure to ensure a clear path before crossing the centerline may result in a head-on crash with an approaching vehicle.

- *Passing vehicles in a no passing zone* -- No passing zones often are so designated because there is a limited sight distance for vehicles approaching in the opposite direction. Failure to respect this situation may result in the apparatus colliding head-on with an approaching vehicle. It also may force the vehicle being passed off the roadway.

- *Passing vehicles on their right side* -- Reports show that on occasion fire apparatus drivers attempt to pass stopped or slowed vehicles on that vehicle's right side. This is dangerous because all civilian drivers are told to move over to the right when they recognize that an emergency vehicle is approaching. In some cases the civilian driver will panic at first and come to a dead stop wherever he or she is. Then the driver will suddenly remember the old rule and move to the right. If the

Figure 1-6 Fire apparatus should never pass another vehicle on its right side.

apparatus is in the process of passing that vehicle on its right side, a crash may occur **(Figure 1-6)**. See section on right-of-way issues for additional information.

- *Going the wrong way on a one-way street* -- In order to avoid going around the block, the apparatus may be driven the wrong way up a one-way street. If total control of the street cannot be ensured, a head-on crash with a legally operated vehicle may occur.

- *Driving in the wrong direction on a limited-access highway* -- In some cases it may be necessary to access a crash or fire scene on a limited-access highway by traveling in the wrong lanes of that roadway. This should only be done if law enforcement personnel can ensure that those lanes have been closed to oncoming traffic. Otherwise a head-on crash may occur.

- *Traversing an activated railroad crossing* -- Apparatus crashes have occurred in situations where the driver of the fire apparatus failed to yield to an activated railroad crossing. In other cases, the apparatus driver will fail to come to a complete stop and check in both directions before traversing a railroad crossing that is not equipped with lights or crossing arms. The end result is a train versus fire apparatus crash in which the train will be the victor on every occasion.

Driver training programs must reinforce the need to follow posted traffic regulations as much as possible. Information on exceptions granted to emergency vehicles by State motor vehicle codes and the circumstances in which these exceptions may be exercised also should be covered.

Failure to Yield Right-of-Way by Civilian Drivers

Not all of the human factors that result in tanker crashes are attributable to the driver of the tanker. In some cases, civilian drivers operate their vehicles in a reckless, irresponsible, or otherwise improper manner leading to a crash involving the fire apparatus. The fire apparatus may collide with the offending vehicle, or it will crash trying to avoid the offending vehicle. Some of the more common problems caused by civilian drivers include:

1. Unpredictable behavior created by a panic reaction to an approaching emergency vehicle
2. Failure to obey posted traffic regulations or directions
3. Failure to stop for a red signal light or stop sign
4. Failure to yield the right-of-way to emergency vehicles
5. Excessive speed
6. Inattentiveness or inability to hear approaching emergency vehicles because of vehicle air conditioning, loud music, etc.

Fire apparatus drivers must always be cognizant of the fact that they have little control over the way members of the public react toward them. With this in mind, drivers must always drive defensively and never put themselves, or the public, in a situation where there is no alternative (other than crashing into each other). There is virtually no action by a civilian driver that cannot be compensated for in a manner that will avoid a crash if the fire apparatus is driven cautiously and defensively.

Fire departments, in their public fire education programs, may wish to include information on proper driving techniques for civilians who are being approached by emergency vehicles. By better educating the public on how to react properly when encountering an emergency response, potential hazards to both the public and emergency responders can be noticeably reduced.

APPARATUS DESIGN FACTORS

The second group of factors that are commonly found to be at least partially involved in the cause of fire department tankers are apparatus design factors. The design of the apparatus may be the major factor leading to the incident. However, in reality, some human factor is generally involved as well. Even if the apparatus does have some design or mechanical design issues, cautious and appropriate operation by the driver can usually overcome these.

Apparatus design factors that lead to a crash are most commonly associated with inadequacies associated with home-built or modified apparatus. This is not always the case, however. Even custom-built fire apparatus, conforming to Department of Transportation (DOT) and NFPA requirements, have characteristics that may contribute to a crash. This section will explore the most common apparatus design factors that can contribute to fire department tanker crashes.

Weight of Apparatus

Quite commonly, fire department tankers are the heaviest apparatus to be operated by any particular fire department (**Figure 1-7**). Straight-chassis fire department tankers weighing in excess of 25 tons are common. Tractor-trailer tankers may weigh considerably more. Drivers who are driving these vehicles must take the heavy weight of these apparatus into account.

Figure 1-7 Fire department tankers are very large, heavy vehicles. *Courtesy of Joel Woods, Maryland Fire & Rescue Institute*

The driver must remember that the tanker does not handle the same, or stop as fast, as the privately owned vehicle he or she drove to the fire station. Because of the huge weight difference, it takes a much greater distance for a fire apparatus to stop than does a smaller passenger vehicle. The brake systems used on fire apparatus may take a little longer to activate and stop a vehicle than do the brake systems on smaller passenger vehicles. Because of these factors, drivers must be reminded that following distances and speed that they maintain in their private vehicles, or even smaller fire apparatus, will not be sufficient for safe operation of the tanker. In most cases, their following distances must be increased and the speed decreased in order to operate the vehicle safely.

The heavy weight of the apparatus may also be a factor on marginal driving surfaces. Surfaces that safely carry the weight of smaller vehicles may give way under the extreme load imposed by a tanker. This is particularly true toward the edge of a road's surface. If the tanker's right wheels get too close to the edge of a weak road surface, that surface may crumble or otherwise fracture. This could immediately cause the apparatus to begin a rolling motion toward the right. In other cases, the driver might overcorrect in trying to get the wheels back on the driving surface. This often results in the apparatus shooting across the opposite lanes of traffic or beginning a rolling action in the opposite direction. More information of dealing with these situations is contained later in this document.

Age of Apparatus

Numerous investigations have attributed part of the cause of a crash to excessive age of the apparatus. Fire apparatus tend to deteriorate with age and the associated wear and tear that comes with it. If the apparatus deteriorates past the point of being safe, it may lead to a crash.

Age of the apparatus alone generally is not the factor responsible for a crash. In most cases where age is cited as a crash factor, it is really a combination of age and improper maintenance that leads to the problem. Properly maintained apparatus may still be in a safe condition after many years of service. However, in many jurisdictions, there is a tendency not to pay as much attention to the care of older apparatus, especially if they are reserve apparatus or are not used on a frequent basis. Thus, when the apparatus is placed into service, a mechanical failure occurs and age is cited as the reason. In reality, it was the combination of age, poor maintenance, and metal fatigue that led to the failure.

The age of the apparatus could be a crash factor even if the apparatus has been perfectly maintained and is in "normal" operating condition. Suppose the fire department operates a fleet of modern apparatus, equipped with all the latest features including power steering and antilock, air-operated brakes. The exception to this rule is the 30-year-old tanker that the department maintains for those rare instances when a fire occurs outside the hydranted area of its response district. The older tanker does not have power steering and is equipped with mechanical/hydraulic brakes. If the driver of the tanker does not recognize the different handling characteristics of the older tanker (harder to turn, increased stopping distance, etc.), a crash may be the result, even though the apparatus was functioning as designed. In this case, proper operation of the tanker was so different from that of the newer apparatus that the failure to recognize this difference could be cited as a crash factor.

High Center of Gravity

The further away from the ground that the vehicle's center of gravity is, the less stable that vehicle will become **(Figure 1-8)**. Vehicles that have a high center of gravity are often referred to as "top heavy." Vehicles that are top heavy are more severely affected by quick turns and maneuvers than are vehicles with lower centers of gravity. In addition to tankers, there are several other types of fire department vehicles that have been known to have high centers of gravity and the problems that result from this condition. These vehicles include aircraft rescue and firefighting (ARFF) vehicles, aerial apparatus, brush fire apparatus, command vehicles, ambulances, and even some fire department pumpers.

Vehicles that have a high center of gravity are dangerous from several standpoints related to the driver's ability to control the vehicle. Top-heavy vehicles have a tendency to want to tip over if they are driven through a curve at an unsafe speed. This tendency is a matter of simple physics involving inertia and momentum. As the vehicle negotiates the turn in one direction, momentum and inertia cause the weight of the vehicle to lean in the opposite direction to which the vehicle is turning (in reality *toward* the same direction the vehicle was traveling before the curve was started). If the speed of the vehicle is too great, this inertia may cause the vehicle to leave the road or roll over toward the outside of the curve **(Figure 1-9)**.

Figure 1-8 Some tankers, by design, have a high center of gravity. *Courtesy of Ron Bogardus*

Even if the vehicle does not roll over, this inertia going away from the direction the vehicle is being driven may result in the vehicle's tires losing a solid grip with the road surface. This could result in a skid or slide that leads to a crash if the driver is unable to correct it.

The problems associated with a high center of gravity are magnified when dealing with tankers because of the large amount of weight the vehicles carry. Again, simple physics dictates that the forces of a momentum arm are increased if the arm is lengthened or the weight at the end of the arm is increased. In the case of a fire apparatus, the momentum arm extends from the road surface to the apparatus' center of gravity. While the length of the momentum arm associated with a tanker may be no longer than that of a pumper or aerial apparatus, certainly in most cases the weight at the center of gravity will be considerably greater for the tanker (**Figure 1-10**). If the center of gravity is too high, this greater weight will increase the tanker's tendency to want to turn over when driven under the same conditions as the lighter vehicles.

Design of New Fire Apparatus

Issues related to apparatus design are not limited to home-built or retrofitted apparatus. In many cases, new apparatus have design elements that may make them susceptible to being involved in a crash from the time they are delivered from the factory. Most fire apparatus manufacturers do a fine job of adhering to DOT and NFPA requirements for apparatus design. However, one must keep in mind that those standards and regulations are considered to be *minimum* standards. Vehicles that meet these requirements may still have

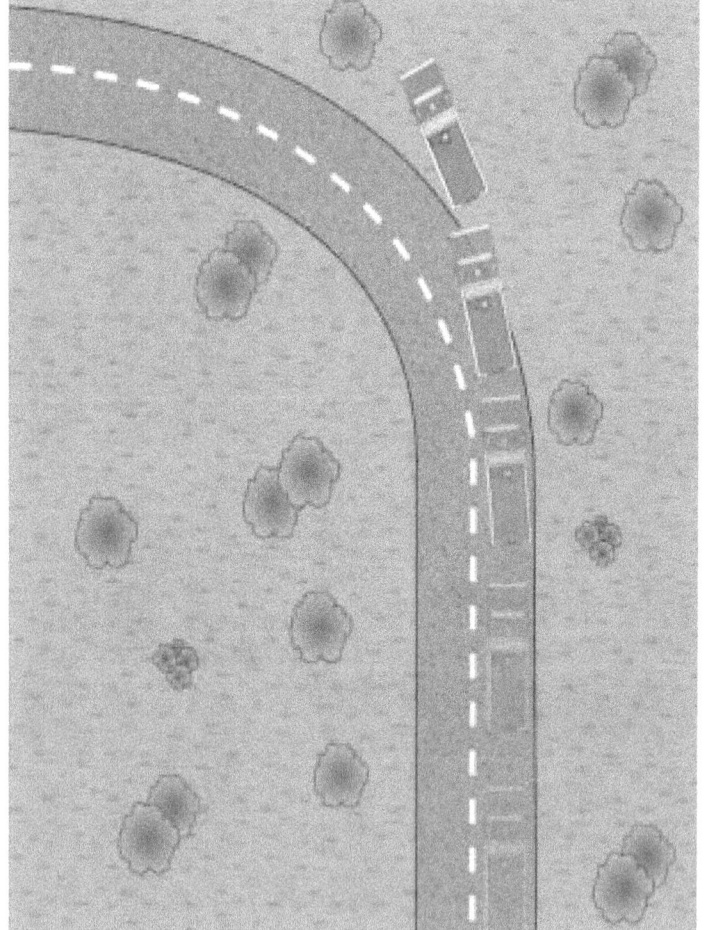

Figure 1-9 Inertia may cause the tanker to exit the roadway to the outside of the curve.

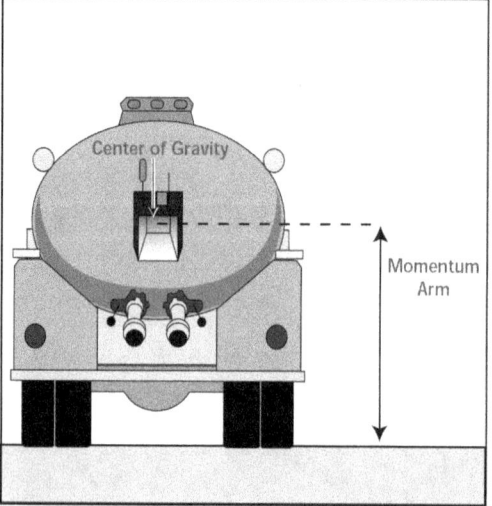

Figure 1-10 The arm extends from the tanker's momentum center of gravity down to the road surface.

SAFE OPERATION OF FIRE TANKERS

some characteristics, such as a high center of gravity, that makes the vehicle more susceptible to being involved in a crash. In other cases, in order to suit the specifications of the fire department purchasing the vehicle, the manufacturer may end up building an apparatus that has some inherent design disadvantages.

One of the most common design problems associated with new apparatus is a vehicle that is over its legal weight. In order to suit the purchaser's desire to carry a specified amount of personnel, water, and equipment, the result may be a vehicle that has too much weight to be safely carried by the chassis, axles, and braking system of the apparatus. While it is not always an accurate indicator, these overweight vehicles are often visible to the naked eye. Apparatus that have an unusual amount of sagging on their rear ends are often overweight. Overweight vehicles are more susceptible to steering, braking, and other problems than vehicles of legal weight.

One of the most common weight-related design problems associated with fire department tankers is trying to carry too much water on a specific chassis. Pumper-tankers and square-side tankers equipped with T-shaped water tanks on a single rear-axle chassis should carry no more than 1,500 gallons of water **(Figure 1-11)**. Single rear axle chassis equipped with elliptical water tanks should be limited to about 2,000 gallons of water **(Figure 1-12)**. Tankers with a tandem rear axle are generally limited to about 4,000 gallons of water **(Figure 1-13)**. All of these figures will vary depending on the gross vehicle weight rating of the chassis, the type of fire pump (if any) carried on the apparatus, and the amount of hose and other equipment expected to be carried on the apparatus.

Another common design disadvantage is a vehicle with an excessively high center of gravity. The hazards of a high center of gravity were discussed in the previous section. New apparatus tend to have excessively high centers of

Figure 1-11 Tankers with T-shaped tanks and single rear axles should be limited to 1,500 gallons of water. *Courtesy of Ron Bogardus*

Figure 1-12 Tankers with elliptical tanks and single rear axles should be limited to 2,000 gallons of water.

Figure 1-13 Straight chassis, tandem-axle tankers may carry as much as 4,000 gallons of water.

CAUSES OF FIRE DEPARTMENT TANKER CRASHES

gravity when the apparatus is built with a shorter wheelbase than that which would be normally used for the amount of water and equipment to be carried on the apparatus. Fire departments often specify restricted wheelbases because of space limitations in the fire station (**Figure 1-14**). In other cases, the shorter wheelbase is intended to assist vehicle maneuvering in congested response districts.

To exemplify this problem, consider the following scenario. Suppose that a pumper-tanker that carries 3,000 gallons of water normally ends up being 35 feet long. However, the purchasing fire department wishes to locate a new 3,000-gallon pumper-tanker in a fire station that limits the length of the vehicle to 30 feet. Apparatus manufacturers are able to find a way to put

Figure 1-14 Tankers with shortened wheelbases tend to have higher centers of gravity. *Courtesy of Ron Jeffers*

all the features the fire department wants on a vehicle that is 5 feet shorter. However, because expanding the vehicle's width is not practical, the vehicle will have to be designed to be taller than the standard apparatus. A shorter, taller vehicle translates into a higher center of gravity. It can also result in a vehicle that does not meet Federal bridge gross weight requirements. These requirements are detailed in Chapter 4 of this document.

Improper Modification of Apparatus

In some circumstances, perfectly safe, well-designed fire apparatus are turned unsafe when the owner modifies the apparatus. Common examples of this scenario include

- The fire department decides to add a considerable amount of heavy equipment to an existing apparatus.

- The fire department increases the size and capacity of the vehicle's existing water tank.

- The fire department changes the function of an apparatus by significantly modifying the body of the apparatus. An example would be changing an aerial apparatus into a tanker by removing the aerial body and equipment and replacing it with a tanker body.

These changes or added weight may push the vehicle over its designed or legal weight limit. The result is often a crash that occurs because of a mechanical failure or the inability of the vehicle's braking system to stop the vehicle before a crash occurs.

There is an old adage that states "you can pay me now, or pay me later." Well-intentioned efforts to save money when retrofitting an apparatus may end up costing the department significantly more money when some type of accident or failure occurs. These additional costs sometimes end up equaling or exceeding the cost of having the work professionally done or a new apparatus being purchased. More unfortunately, in some cases the additional costs are in terms of human injury and death.

Retrofitting of Non-Fire Service Apparatus

Records show that a large percentage of serious crashes involving fire department tankers can be attributed to tankers that were crafted from non-fire service vehicles. In some cases, the "new" tanker is placed on a government surplus vehicle that is already in questionable mechanical condition. In other cases, a reliable vehicle chassis is obtained and then an excessive amount of weight is added to it.

Fire departments with limited financial resources often craft tankers out of surplus government vehicles. Military 6x6 transport vehicles, forestry trucks, and aircraft servicing vehicles are the most common to be converted into fire department tankers (**Figures 1-15 a & b**). Fire department administrators should remember that generally the reason these vehicles are made available through surplus equipment programs is because the vehicles have exhausted their usefulness to the agency that was operating them. This is a nice way to say that the vehicles are worn out and their previous owners no longer wish to deal with their maintenance issues. Thus, fire departments that acquire these vehicles are often beginning with vehicles that are in a questionable mechanical and safety condition. If these mechanical issues are not dealt with as a part of the retrofitting process, the department may be placing a very dangerous vehicle into service. The danger of these flaws may be multiplied by placing a large water tank on the vehicle. The added weight to the vehicle may accelerate the failure of part of the apparatus.

Figure 1-15a A military 6x6 vehicle converted into a fire department tanker.

Another common practice is to develop a fire department tanker using a converted fuel oil or gasoline tanker (**Figure 1-16**). Even though these vehicles may be in excellent condition when the fire department acquires them, these chassis frequently are not designed for the weight of the water

Figure 1-15b A military fuel tanker converted into a fire department tanker.

Figure 1-16 Many fire departments have converted civilian fuel tankers to fire tankers.

that will be carried on them. One gallon of water weighs 8.33 pounds. One gallon of gasoline weighs 5.6 pounds, and one gallon of fuel oil weighs 7.12 pounds. Thus, if the vehicle's tank holds 2,000 gallons, water will weigh 5,460 pounds more than gasoline and 2,420 pounds more than fuel oil. This added weight creates significant safety issues for the vehicle.

Another problem with converting fuel tankers is that in many cases the liquid tanks are improperly baffled for fire department use. These vehicles are often designed to be driven completely full or completely empty. Thus, when the vehicle is being driven with a partially filled tank, liquid surges within the tank can result in the vehicle going out of control.

Figure 1-17 Pumps and piping can add a considerable amount of weight to the apparatus.

Another weight-related issue commonly found on retrofit tankers is the addition of pumps, piping, and other associated equipment to the apparatus (**Figure 1-17**). This equipment may further complicate the overweight problems discussed above. The weight of equipment must be considered along with the weight of water when determining the safe carrying capacity of the equipment.

Tankers that formerly hauled food products, such as milk, commonly do not have any baffles in the tank. This is because baffles make the tank extremely difficult to properly clean and sanitize. Fire departments considering converting these vehicles for emergency use must add baffles or baffle balls to the inside of the tank before placing them in service (**Figures 1-18 a & b**).

Regardless of the commodity that the tanker previously was designed to haul, another significant impact of the wear and tear on the vehicle is that milk and fuel tankers generally only spend a fraction of every 24-hour period with a full tank. When parked and not in use they most commonly have empty tanks. Fire department tankers are loaded with water 24 hours a day, every day. This constant load on the chassis and suspension will increase the amount of wear on the apparatus once it is converted to a fire tanker.

Figure 1-18a A baffle ball. *Courtesy of Snow Equipment Sales*

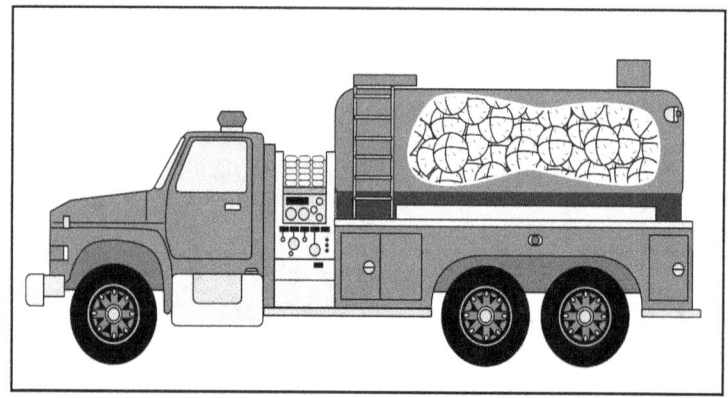

Figure 1-18b Baffle balls are inserted into the tank through the tank vent. *Courtesy of Snow Equipment Sales*

Liquid Surge

The problems associated with improperly baffled water tanks have been discussed in several of the sections above. Because they have shown to be a causal factor in a significant number of fire department tanker crashes, it is worthy of a more detailed analysis.

NFPA 1901, *Standard for Automotive Fire Apparatus*, contains specific requirements for the proper baffling of water and foam concentrate tanks on fire department tankers. In short, baffles are strategically placed divider walls inside the water or foam concentrate tank. These dividers are intended to prevent the liquid in the tank from sloshing front-to-back or side-to-side when the vehicle is in motion. More details on proper baffling are contained in Chapter 4 of this report.

Liquid surge results from the movement of liquid in a partially full, unbaffled tank. There are two common times when liquid surge becomes a problem. The first is when the vehicle changes directions, such as when negotiating a curve in the road. If the vehicle enters the curve too fast, centrifugal force will cause the liquid in the tank to surge against the wall of the vehicle on the outside of the curve. In severe situations, this surge can be sufficient to push the vehicle off the roadway or cause it to roll over. If the vehicle is also overly top heavy, the chances of a rollover are even greater.

Liquid surges can also be troublesome when the driver attempts to stop the vehicle rapidly. When the vehicle's brakes are applied hastily, the liquid surges toward the front of the tank **(Figure 1-19)**. This additional force surging forward can further increase the stopping distance of the vehicle. Once the vehicle comes to a stop, the liquid in the tank will continue to slosh back and forth in the tank. On slippery road surfaces, this could cause the vehicle to be pushed forward into an intersection or a railroad crossing.

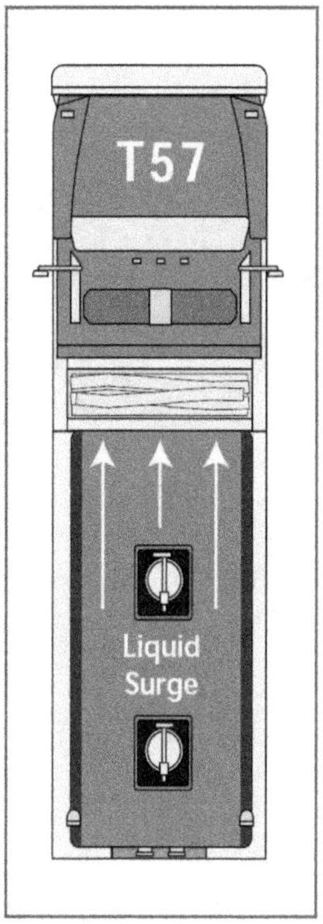

Figure 1-19 Liquid surge can work to propel the vehicle forward.

Poor Apparatus Maintenance

Poor maintenance of apparatus can result in vehicle system failures that lead to crashes. This is particularly true of braking systems. Several of the fatal fire apparatus crashes covered in the case history section of this report had their causes traced back to improperly maintained apparatus braking systems. The dangers associated with faulty brakes, or for that matter any improperly maintained vehicle system, are accentuated by the heavy weight of a tanker. Failures will usually occur faster and more dramatically the heavier a vehicle is. By following an effective apparatus maintenance program using certified mechanics, the likelihood of mechanical failure leading to crash can be reduced. Detailed information on establishing an effective apparatus maintenance program can be found in Chapter 4 of this report.

DRIVING SURFACE FACTORS

Up to this point we have focused on crash causes that may be controlled by the driver or the fire department. Unfortunately, not every factor that causes fire department tanker crashes is within the driver's control. One such factor is the surface on which the vehicle is being driven. There is little the fire department can do to improve the condition of the roads in its response area.

There are a variety of driving surface factors that may increase the likelihood of a crash occurring. It must be noted, however, that virtually every adverse road surface condition can be compensated for by a properly trained driver who drives the vehicle appropriately for the given conditions.

This section explores some of the more common adverse driving surface conditions that have historically been noted in fire department tanker crash investigations. Techniques for safely driving fire department tankers over these adverse conditions are covered in detail in Chapter 4 of this report.

Poor Road Design

In some cases, the actual driving surface may be in satisfactory condition, but the design of the road is such that it creates a hazard for vehicles driving on it. Some examples of situations like this are:

- *Roads with high center crowns* -- Roads are often designed with a crown in the middle to facilitate water runoff during rainy weather. However, sometimes the center crown of the road is so elevated that vehicles driving on it have a considerable amount of lean toward the outside of the road **(Figure 1-20)**. This makes it more difficult to handle any vehicle driven on that surface. It is particularly hazardous for tankers with improper baffling or high centers of gravity. The outward lean of the driving surface will increase the vehicle's tendency to want to tip over.

Figure 1-20 An excessive crown on the road may tend to cause the tanker to lean towards the shoulder.

- *Curves that are banked toward the outside of the turn* -- Again, in order to facilitate adequate drainage of the road surface, curves in the roadway are often banked. As long as the road is banked toward the inside of the curve, like turns on a racetrack, this does not create any significant hazard. In fact, inward-facing curves increase the safety of a vehicle moving on the curve as they help to counteract the tendency of centrifugal force to push the vehicle toward the outside. On the other hand, if the roadway is banked toward the outside of the turn, the vehicle is more likely to become unstable and overturn because of the combined force of the outward lean and centrifugal force.

- *Curves that are not banked at all* -- Flat curves are nearly as problematic as curves that are banked toward the outside of the turn. Flat curves will not assist the apparatus in overcoming centrifugal forces or in the tires maintaining contact with the road surface. Flat curves require the apparatus operator to slow the apparatus to avoid sliding off the road surface.

- *Roads that are unable to support the weight of heavy fire apparatus* -- Some roadways are not designed to support the weight of heavy vehicles. These types of roads may be found in private residential developments, commercial or industrial properties, or rural areas. The road surface may be a thin layer of asphalt laid directly over light grade gravel **(Figure 1-21)**. While these surfaces are more than adequate for supporting passenger vehicles and light duty trucks, frequently they are inadequate for heavy trucks such as fire apparatus. When the apparatus drives onto one of these surfaces, the potential for breaking the surface and bogging down occurs. If only one side of the apparatus punches through the surface, a rollover situation could occur. Be particularly alert for these types of surfaces during periods of hot weather. The hot weather weakens asphalt and may be the factor that allows a marginal driving surface to fail.

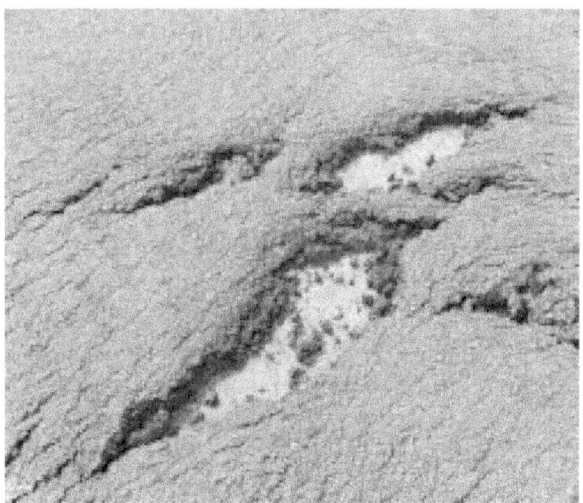

Figure 1-21 Some road surfaces do not stand up to the weight of heavy fire apparatus.

Fire departments should assess their response districts to determine roads that pose potential hazards. These thoroughfares should be noted in preincident planning and fire department response route policies. When possible, roads of questionable design should be avoided. If it is not possible to avoid the routes, drivers should be cognizant of the hazards they pose and operate the vehicle accordingly.

Severe Grades

Roads that contain severe grades, whether they be uphill or downhill grades, pose challenges for drivers of fire department tankers. Of the two, severe downhill grades pose the greatest amount of danger. The influence of gravity on the vehicle creates the tendency for the vehicle to accelerate as it travels down grade. Unless the driver exercises appropriate safety measures (shifting to a lower gear, applying the brakes periodically, etc.), the vehicle may reach speeds that render it uncontrollable. This can result in a number of consequences, such as being unable to negotiate a curve at the bottom of the hill or striking a vehicle or other object because of the inability to stop the vehicle.

Uphill grades also challenge the driver, particularly when driving apparatus equipped with a manual transmission. As the apparatus climbs the grade, the drivetrain labors increasingly to keep the vehicle moving. In most cases it will be necessary to shift the vehicle into a lower gear in order to continue forward progress. Should the driver miss or slip a gear during the shifting process, he or she may be unable to get the apparatus back into gear. Eventually, the vehicle's forward progress will stop and the vehicle could begin to roll backwards. The rolling vehicle could strike other vehicles following the laboring apparatus too closely.

Sharp Curves

Sharp curves in and of themselves are not a danger. The danger factor is added when the driver attempts to guide the apparatus through the curve at an excessive speed. If the inertia of the vehicle exceeds the tires' ability to hold the road surface, the vehicle will slide off the road and/or roll over. Drivers should be aware of all sharp curves in their response area and the maximum speeds at which they may be safely negotiated by a tanker. The speed will need to be reduced even further when the road surface is wet or icy.

Figure 1-22 Many road signs indicating a curve are accompanied by a suggested maximum speed limit.

In many cases, the highway department posts yellow signs that warn drivers of an approaching sharp curve. A smaller sign that lists a suggested reduced speed through the curve is often located beneath the primary sign (**Figure 1-22**). The suggested speed on these signs is intended for *passenger cars* under ideal, dry road conditions. The speeds on these signs may be too high for safe negotiation by larger vehicles, including fire department tankers. Drivers of all large fire department vehicles, including tankers, must consider these "suggested" speeds as the absolute maximum for their vehicles. They must adjust accordingly when driving in less than ideal conditions or when the characteristics of the apparatus make the suggested speed unsafe. The case studies covered later in the report will show several instances where these signs were ignored and fatal crashes occurred.

Unimproved Road Surfaces

The term *unimproved road surfaces* is used to describe roads that have not been paved with a hard surface such as asphalt or concrete. Unimproved road surfaces include dirt, gravel, sand, stone, and similar road materials. Unimproved road surfaces can be hazardous for vehicles of any size and weight. The heavy weight of fire department tankers magnifies the dangers posed by these roads. Some of the prevalent hazards of unimproved road surfaces include

Figure 1-23 Be alert for signs that a road may be subject to washouts.

- *Instability of the road surface* -- The road may have sections that wash out or become otherwise impassible after heavy rainfalls (**Figure 1-23**). Should the apparatus be unable to avoid a washed-out section, the apparatus may be forced off the road surface and overturn. In other circumstances, the road may simply be weakened by weather conditions or heavy vehicle traffic. When the heavy tanker travels across the weakened area, the road surface gives way beneath the tanker.

- *Rough road surfaces* -- Unimproved roads typically contain numerous bumps, potholes, and other deformities **(Figure 1-24)**. Apparatus that strike these deformities while traveling at an unsafe speed may be difficult for the driver/operator to control. The sudden jar of the bump or pothole may throw the vehicle to one side or the other. If the vehicle bounces as a result of the jar, it may be difficult to steer or brake, causing the vehicle to go into a slide. Of particular danger are dirt and gravel roads that contain sections with a series of ridges that create a "washboard" effect. Vehicles that traverse these sections of washboard will begin a rhythmic bouncing that will reduce the driver's ability to steer and/or slow the vehicle. The vehicle may go into an uncontrollable skid caused by the loss of contact with the road surface. Or, this bouncing may damage the tire or the wheel and result in a blowout or slow leak leading to a flat tire.

Figure 1-24 Unpaved roads may contain serious deformities.

- *Reduced tire traction* -- The actual driving surface of an unimproved road is usually either loose dirt or gravel. Each of these provides limited traction, particularly when attempting to stop the vehicle. Even vehicles with anti-skid braking systems are more susceptible to skids on these loose road surfaces. Vehicles that strike a bump or pothole -- as described in the previous paragraph -- are more susceptible to skids on these surfaces because there is less traction for the tires to prevent sideward movement of the vehicle.

- *Mud* -- Dirt roads can become more problematic following periods of precipitation. Depending on the type of soil and quality of the road to begin with, the result can range from the road becoming more slippery to being completely impassable. If the muddy road has a center crown, there will be a tendency for the vehicle to slide toward the shoulder, which often contains a ditch. In severe cases, the road may become so soft that the weight of the tanker causes it to sink and become stuck.

- *Reduced visibility* -- Quite the opposite from the problems created by muddy roads are those created by roads that have been exposed to prolonged periods of dry weather. Dry unimproved roads tend to produce large quantities of dust when vehicles drive over them. This dust can remain suspended in the air for a considerable amount of time and can severely reduce visibility for drivers of vehicles that enter into the cloud. At times, visibility can be reduced to zero. This reduced visibility could cause the driver to be unable to determine his or her exact position on the road. The results can include driving the vehicle off the road surface, crossing the center of the road and striking another vehicle head-on, or driving into the rear of a slower moving or stopped vehicle.

Fire departments should identify unimproved road surfaces in their pre-incident planning activities. Roads that are particularly unstable or subject to extended periods of muddiness should be identified. When possible, unimproved roads should be avoided for emergency responses. It may be safer, and even faster, to take a paved road to an emergency scene, even if that route is slightly longer, than using the unimproved road. Drivers must be trained to exercise additional caution when driving on unimproved roads following periods of rain or extended dry weather.

Adverse Weather Conditions

Numerous fire department tanker crashes over the years have been attributed to loss of control of the vehicle while driving during adverse weather conditions. Adverse weather conditions include rain, ice, snow, and fog. There are two primary hazards associated with adverse weather conditions: reduced road surface traction and reduced visibility.

Water, snow, and ice on the road surface each reduce the vehicle's ability to secure maximum traction. Of those three, water will have the least impact on traction and ice or hard-packed snow will have the greatest. All three must be respected and compensated for by the driver of the tanker. According to IFSTA, the addition of any form of precipitation to the road surface may increase the vehicle's safe stopping distance by anywhere from 3 to 15 times the distance required to stop the same vehicle on a dry surface. Drivers must compensate for this by slowing down and increasing their following distance behind other vehicles.

Fog, blowing snow, and heavy rain can also severely reduce the driver's ability to see a safe distance in front of the vehicle. The hazards associated with reduced visibility were described above in the section on dusty unimproved roads. Drivers must also compensate for these conditions by slowing down and increasing their following distance behind other vehicles. They should also avoid the use of high-beam headlights and reduce the amount or intensity of warning lights being used in order to cut down on the amount of light reflected back toward the apparatus driver.

Figure 1-25 Be alert for paved roads that do not have paved shoulders.

Lack of/Soft Road Shoulders

As this report will detail in the chapters to follow, one of the most common causes for serious fire department tanker crashes is overcorrection by the driver when the vehicle's right side tires leave the roadway. Roadways that are not accompanied by paved shoulders outside of the driving lanes serve many jurisdictions (**Figure 1-25**). If a vehicle traveling on this type of road moves too far to the right, the vehicle's right side tires can leave the road's surface. Typically there is a drop-off of several inches or more where the paved surface ends. Drivers get into trouble when they attempt to return the vehicle to the paved surface by quickly turning the steering wheel toward the left while still traveling at a high rate of speed. Often the result of this action is the vehicle lurching severely toward the left when the right side wheels jump back onto the paved surface. This may cause the tanker to travel into oncoming lanes of traffic, travel completely over to the opposite side of the roadway, or to simply overturn. Procedures for dealing with this situation are detailed in Chapter 4.

Some roads that do not have paved shoulders may have dirt shoulders built up to the road's surface. If the ground is dry, hard, and compact, these dirt shoulders may eliminate some of the hazards described in the previous paragraph. However, if the dirt shoulders are not in good condition, the heavy weight of a tanker could cause the vehicle to sink into the ground should the right side tires leave the paved roadway. The result will be the same as if the road had no shoulder at all.

Limited Weight Capacity Bridges

Though not a common cause of fire department tanker crashes, limited weight capacity bridges must be considered as a potential hazardous driving surface factor. Many jurisdictions, particularly rural ones, have thoroughfares that include bridges with weight limit restrictions **(Figure 1-26)**. Weight restrictions are imposed on bridges that are of lightweight construction, old, or in poor condition. In many cases, the maximum posted weight for these bridges is considerably less than the weight of a fire department tanker.

Figure 1-26 Always heed bridge weight limit restrictions.

Even in emergency situations, never drive a fire department tanker over a bridge whose weight restriction is less than the weight of the apparatus. The chance of a bridge collapse is significant in these situations. Fire departments should identify these bridges in pre-incident plans and response SOP's. Alternative routes around these bridges must be used whenever possible. In other cases, it may be preferable to summon mutual aid from the other side of the bridge.

EMERGENCY SCENE FACTORS

To this point in the chapter, the content has generally focused on the causes of fire department tanker crashes during road travel (including the response and returning to quarters). On occasion fire department tankers are involved in crashes while operating at the emergency scene itself. These crashes may be a result of maneuvering the apparatus at the emergency or by being struck by another vehicle while parked. This section highlights some of the more common types of incident scene crashes.

Emergency Scene Congestion

A significant portion of fire department tanker crashes that occur on the emergency scene can be attributed to congestion of the scene. The immediate area around an emergency incident may be cluttered and congested prior to the arrival of the first emergency vehicle. Sources of this congestion include

- narrow streets, roads, and lanes;

- parked vehicles;

- utility poles, signs, and trees;

- bystanders;

- backed-up vehicular traffic; and

- debris from the incident itself (wrecked cars, fallen building materials) **(Figure 1-27)**.

Figure 1-27 In some cases, roads near the incident scene may be choked with debris.

As if the potential obstacles listed above were not enough, the response of emergency personnel to the scene only adds to the congestion. In particular, poor positioning of initially arriving emergency vehicles can greatly affect and restrict the movement and positioning of later-arriving vehicles. Because tankers are usually not the first emergency vehicles to arrive on the scene of an incident, some of the added congestion that drivers of these vehicles may encounter include

- police or other non-fire department responder vehicles;

- ambulances or other EMS vehicles;

- earlier-arriving fire apparatus (engines, aerial apparatus, rescue companies, command vehicles, etc.);

- hoselines laid or portable water tanks deployed by earlier-arriving fire apparatus **(Figure 1-28)**; and

- personal vehicles driven to the scene by volunteer or call-back firefighters (the impact of this can be lessened by requiring all of these vehicles to park on the same side of the street).

Figure 1-28 Water tanks and hoses can easily block access to a scene if proper planning in their placement is not used.

Tanker drivers, particularly those with little experience or training, may find it extremely difficult to maneuver such a large apparatus around all of these obstacles. During a period of adrenaline-driven haste, the driver may attempt to squeeze the tanker into a scene where it will not fit. This may result in a crash with one of the obstacles, or worse, with other personnel on the scene. As will be seen later in this report, cramming a tanker into a congested incident scene is unsafe, and poor from a firefighting tactical standpoint. Once the tanker is squeezed into the scene, it becomes boxed in or slowed should another load of water be needed.

Oncoming Traffic at the Emergency Scene

While it would always be the first choice to close all roadways around an incident scene, this is not always possible. In some cases, the incident may be on a major highway that cannot be shut down. In other cases, such as EMS calls or small fires, the activity at the scene does not warrant completely closing the street. Regardless of the situation, any time the fire apparatus is exposed to moving civilian vehicular traffic, the threat of a crash is very real.

Civilian drivers are prone to poor decisions and errors when passing an emergency scene. A review of previous onscene fire apparatus crashes shows that the following causes of crashes by civilian drivers are somewhat common:

- In an effort to determine the nature of the emergency incident, the driver takes his or her eyes off the road and strikes an emergency vehicle or oncoming traffic.

- Excessive emergency vehicle warning and floodlights blind the driver during nighttime operations.

- Annoyed by the delay of a traffic backup, the driver travels through the scene too fast and causes a crash.

The tanker driver should always try to position the apparatus in a manner that minimizes its exposure to oncoming traffic as much as possible. The exception to this rule is when it will be required for emergency responders to work on or near the roadway. In these situations, the apparatus should be positioned between oncoming traffic and the responders to act as a shield. Detailed information on appropriate apparatus placement relative to oncoming traffic is discussed in Chapter 4 of this manual.

Maneuvering at Water Shuttle Fill/Dump Sites

One of the most common tactical uses for fire department tankers is to shuttle loads of water between a supply location, called the fill site, and the emergency scene, referred to as the dump site. Both of these sites tend to be rather congested with emergency apparatus, hose and appliances, portable water tanks, and personnel. In some cases, the need to maneuver the tanker into the necessary position increases the likelihood of a crash. Crashes at water shuttle fill and dump sites typically fall into the category of being relatively minor in damage. They are low speed events that generally result in minor bumps, dents, and scrapes to the apparatus. The exception to this is when a firefighter gets caught between the maneuvering tanker and another object. Even at low speeds this type of accident can have deadly consequences.

The water shuttle fill site is typically located at either a fire hydrant or a suitable drafting location at a static water supply source. At least one pumper will be stationed at this location and connected to the water supply source in order to speed the filling of the tanker **(Figure 1-29)**. Hoselines are laid out from the pumper in advance of the first tanker's arrival. When the first empty tanker arrives at the fill site, it parks in close proximity to the discharge ends of the hoselines being supplied by the fill site pumper. Connections are quickly made, the tanker's water tank is filled, the hoses are disconnected, and the tanker drives off back to the emergency scene **(Figure 1-30)**. Fill site crashes occur for a variety of reasons, including

- During positioning of the tanker at the fill hoses, the driver maneuvers the apparatus into an object (such as a utility pole, guardrail, etc.).

- When pulling away after the tanker has been filled, the driver pulls out in front of another emergency vehicle or a civilian vehicle that is not anticipating the tanker's departure.

- An empty tanker approaches the fill site at an excessive rate of speed and is unable to stop before hitting the last tanker in the line waiting to be filled.

- The site is wet and/or icy from water that has spilled during the course of operations, and the apparatus skids as it approaches or enters the fill site.

Figure 1-29 A proper fill site has all of the hoses laid out and ready for connection to the tanker.

Figure 1-30 "Make and break" personnel connect the hoses to the tanker at the fill site.

The water shuttle dump site is located somewhere near the emergency scene. The dump site consists of one or more portable water tanks into which the tankers dump their loads **(Figure 1-31)**. Water is then drafted from the tank(s) by a dump site pumper. The dump site pumper can either be the actual apparatus that is supplying attack lines for the fire, or it can be a dedicated water supply unit that relays water to the attack apparatus. The cause of accidents at the dump site are fairly similar to those described for fill site operations. They include

1. During positioning of the tanker to align its dump valve with the portable tank, the driver maneuvers the apparatus into an object such as the water tank, the dump-site pumper, or another tanker in the process of dumping its load.

2. When pulling away after the tanker has been emptied, the driver pulls out in front of another emergency vehicle or a civilian vehicle that is not anticipating the tanker's departure.

3. A full tanker approaches the dump site at an excessive rate of speed and is unable to stop before hitting the last tanker in the line waiting to dump.

Proper fill and dump site operations and safety precautions are also covered in Chapter 4 of this manual.

SEATBELT USE

The bulk of this chapter has focused on the causes of fire department tanker accidents. The purpose of this discussion has been to focus on the safety issues that most greatly influence the tendency of fire department tankers to become involved in crashes. Certainly any discussion relative to safety issues as they affect tanker crashes would not be complete if the issue of passenger restraint or seatbelt use were not reviewed. While the failure of the tanker driver and/or occupants to wear seatbelts is rarely established to be the *cause* of a crash, it is often a mitigating factor in the severity of the *outcome* of the crash.

Figure 1-31 A properly designed dump site should allow for quick dumping and an expedient departure.

In the case histories and statistics that are contained later in this report, you will not see instances where failure to wear a seatbelt was listed as a cause for a crash. Some crash reconstruction specialists have speculated that particular incidents may have occurred after the unrestrained driver of a truck was bounced out of an effective driving position following the initial contact with a bump in the road or another object. In other cases, the driver came out of the seat after an overcorrective action to return a truck to the roadway after the right side wheels had slipped off the edge. No records of this being the primary causal factor in a fire department tanker accident have ever been documented.

On numerous occasions, the failure to wear seatbelts has been determined to be a significant factor in the death of the tanker driver and/or occupant(s). As the case studies will show, tanker drivers and/or occupants being seriously injured or killed after being partially or totally ejected from the vehicle following a crash is a common theme. This occurs despite the fact that information and studies on the benefits of wearing seatbelts have been available for more than 20 years.

The U.S. Department of Transportation (DOT) and the National Highway Traffic Safety Administration (NHTSA) have been compiling data and statistics on seatbelt use for more than 30 years. While they have not reported data specific for fire department tankers, or any fire apparatus for that matter, the information they have reported on all types of vehicles should be considered relevant for fire apparatus. A 1999 DOT report (DOT HS 809 090; available at www.nhtsa.dot.gov) indicates that the proper use of seatbelts by truck occupants reduces the risk of fatal injury by 60 percent and moderate-to-critical injury by 65 percent.

The 1999 DOT report also indicates that 75 percent of all occupants who are totally ejected from a vehicle suffer fatal injuries. In Chapter 2 of this report, it will be shown that this percentage holds true for fire department tanker accidents. While that figure is applied to all types of crashes, seatbelts show their most dramatic effects on safety when rollover crash statistics are reviewed. As mentioned earlier in the chapter, fire department tankers historically have been involved in a high incidence of rollover crashes. DOT records indicate that nearly 80 percent of all fatalities in truck rollover accidents involved the ejection of an unbelted occupant from the vehicle.

These fatalities in rollover accidents are highly preventable. Again, the DOT report shows that 22 percent of all unrestrained occupants involved in a rollover crash are totally ejected from the vehicle. Dramatically, only one percent of properly restrained occupants are totally ejected from the vehicle in a rollover crash. Fire apparatus drivers and firefighters should be reminded of the above facts in these simple terms:

1. *Three out of four people who are ejected from a vehicle will die.*

2. *Eight out of ten fatalities in rollover accidents involve occupant ejection from the vehicle.*

3. *Occupants are 22 times more likely to be thrown from the vehicle in a rollover accident when they are not wearing their seatbelts.*

Fire personnel have no excuse for failing to wear seatbelts when driving or riding on fire apparatus. NFPA 1901 requires all new fire apparatus to be equipped with a proper seatbelt for each riding position. Most States that have vehicle inspection programs for fire apparatus also require seatbelts to be present. Furthermore, since its first adoption in 1987, NFPA 1500 has required all riders on fire apparatus to be seated and belted prior to the movement of the apparatus. Again, many States have enacted mandatory seatbelt usage laws in recent years, and in some cases, they apply to fire apparatus as well as civilian vehicles.

Despite these facts and evidence, the case studies will show that a significant number of fire service personnel still fail to wear seatbelts when riding on the apparatus. In some of the cases reviewed, not only were the occupants not wearing seatbelts, but the vehicles were found to have the seatbelts removed or tucked away beneath the seat cushions. Given the benefits that seatbelts have proved to hold time and time again, these omissions are unforgivable. Fire department leadership must enforce seatbelt usage for all members of the department.

All fire departments must have in place SOP's that require all members riding on the apparatus to be seated and belted any time the vehicle is ready to begin road travel. The driver should not proceed until this fact has been verified. These policies must be enforced strictly. The benefits of adhering to such a policy have been noted numerous times in recent years. Highly publicized apparatus rollover crashes in Los Angeles (California) and Phoenix (Arizona) resulted in the properly seated and belted firefighters walking away relatively unscathed. As seen in the next chapter, many of their fire service counterparts who failed to follow this policy were killed.

CONCLUSION

In this chapter we have conducted a thorough review of the many reasons that fire department tankers are involved in crashes and why the occupants are injured or killed. In general, these causes include human error, poor apparatus design and/or maintenance, poor road conditions, inclement weather, emergency scene factors, and failure to wear seatbelts. It is important to understand why these accidents occur and why they are so serious so that we can begin to put together a program for reducing their frequency and severity. In the next chapter, we will further examine the problem by applying a statistical review of fatal crashes to determine which causal factors are most significant.

FIRE DEPARTMENT TANKER CRASH STATISTICS

Much can be gained by performing and reviewing a statistical analysis of any problem. Through this review one can learn valuable information regarding the causes of the crashes and the conditions that were present at the time the crashes occurred. This information, in turn, provides direction in determining strategies to help prevent these incidents in the future. Strategies that may become apparent after reviewing these types of statistics include improving driver training, improving apparatus design and construction, better preincident planning, development and enforcement of standard operating procedures SOP's, better maintenance programs, more stringent licensing requirements, and similar necessary measures.

The statistics and case histories featured in this report are limited to fire department tanker crashes between the years 1990 and 2001 that resulted in the fatality of at least one firefighter. Through a variety of sources, including insurance company records, U.S. Fire Administration (USFA) records, U.S. Department of Justice Public Safety Officers' Benefit (PSOB) data, and a variety of other private and governmental sources, 38 fatal crashes involving fire department tankers were identified during that time period. These crashes resulted in the deaths of 42 firefighters. There were 34 crashes that each involved a single fatality and four that each involved two firefighter fatalities.

Certainly, it is realized that for every crash that resulted in a fatality, there were probably a dozen or more that were significant but that did not result in a fatality. Unfortunately, there exists no comprehensive database or data source on these nonfatal crashes. However, the database on fatal incidents is large enough to provide valuable information on the most serious of tanker crashes. Thus, it can be assumed that the information gleaned from these case histories will also be relevant to assessing and preventing nonfatal crashes.

This chapter provides a variety of statistical data regarding fire department tanker crashes. As mentioned above, these data are presented for the purpose of identifying the problem and directing fire service leaders toward strategies for addressing the problem.

TANKER CRASH FREQUENCY

Through data that are provided each year by the USFA and the National Fire Protection Association (NFPA), it is known that approximately 25 percent of all firefighter fatalities occur during traffic crashes. Next to cardiovascular ailments, this is the second largest leading cause of firefighter deaths. It is also a similarly large cause of firefighter injuries. In a report that was jointly developed by the NFPA and the National Institute for Occupational Safety and Health (NIOSH), the types of vehicles that were involved in these fatal crashes were identified. This information can be found in **Table 2-1**.

TABLE 2-1	
Types of Vehicles Involved in Fatal Crashes	
Type of Vehicle	Percentage of Crashes
Firefighters' Personal Vehicles	42.3%
Tankers	21.9%
Engines/Pumpers	20.0%
Ambulance/Rescue Vehicles	6.5%
Others	9.3%
(Source: NFPA)	

The largest category in Table 2-1, firefighters' personal vehicles, can be attributed to volunteer or call-back firefighters who are involved in crashes while responding to or returning from the fire station or incident scene while operating their own vehicles. The fact that this category is so much higher than those for actual emergency vehicles should not be surprising. It is based on simple mathematics and level of risk. For example, if a volunteer fire department gets dispatched for a reported vehicle fire, as many as 10 to 20 firefighters may initiate a response in their personal vehicles. Once at the fire station, a single pumper responds to extinguish the vehicle fire. Thus, the chances of a personal vehicle being involved in a crash in this case was 10 or 20 times greater than the single pumper being involved in one.

When the review is limited to traditional fire department vehicles, tankers account for the largest percentage of crashes. While this fact in and of itself may seem significant, consider that the actual number of tankers in service is the smallest of the three types of vehicles (tankers, pumpers, and ambulance/rescue vehicles) highlighted in the table. The USFA estimates that tankers account for only 3 percent of all fire apparatus in the United States. This dramatizes the need to reinforce tanker operation safety. Perhaps no other statistical information contained in this report more clearly states the problem or need than this one: *while tankers account for only a small percentage of the overall number of vehicles operated by fire departments, they are the most likely type of vehicle to be involved in a fatal crash.*

WHO IS INVOLVED IN TANKER CRASHES?

In the 38 case histories that could be located and reviewed for this report, all of the individuals involved in the crashes were volunteer firefighters. No fatal tanker crashes involving career firefighters were reported during the time period of this study. The fact that volunteer firefighters account for all of these crashes and fatalities should not be a surprise because volunteers generally protect rural areas where tankers are needed.

The areas protected by volunteer firefighters are more likely to be rural and without the benefit of a fixed water supply system than do those protected by career firefighters. Therefore, it must be assumed that although some career fire departments do operate tankers, the overwhelming majority of all fire department tankers in service in the United States are operated by volunteer fire departments. Road conditions in the areas protected by volunteers also tend to be more challenging (more hills, sharp turns, poor road conditions) than those in areas protected by career firefighters. Therefore, it is only natural that volunteers would account for the most crashes involving tankers.

Age and experience may also play a factor in the likelihood of a tanker crash. In the cases that were reviewed, the age group of 20- to 29-year olds accounted for the largest number of fatal tanker crashes. This would tend to show that inexperience might be a significant causal factor in tanker crashes. This is also reflective of standard insurance industry actuary rates for correlating age and crash frequency. A complete accounting of the ages of drivers involved in fatal crashes is contained in **Table 2-2**.

The case histories also revealed that 37 of the 42 firefighters killed in tanker crashes were male **(Table 2-3)**. This figure is probably not overly statistically significant as this also accounts for the approximate percentage of males versus females in the fire service. If there is any significance to this figure, it is to simply state that neither gender has a greater likelihood of being involved in a tanker crash above and beyond the percentage of that gender's representation in the overall fire service.

Lastly, the reports were reviewed to determine where the victims who were fatally injured were riding on the apparatus at the time of the crash **(Table 2-4)**. Approximately three-quarters of the victims were the drivers of the apparatus. This is probably due to the fact that it is quite common for a tanker to respond with only the driver on board. Four of the documented crashes involved the death of both the driver and the right front seat passenger. There were only seven crashes in which the passenger was killed but the driver survived.

The report also documented the States in which these crashes occurred. It was no surprise that States that have expansive rural areas and volunteer fire departments led the list of fatal tanker crashes. A complete listing is contained in Table 2-5.

TABLE 2-4
Seating Position of the Deceased at the Time of the Crash

Seating Position at Time of Crash	Number of Decedents
Driver	31
Right Front Seat	11

TABLE 2-2
Ages of Drivers Involved in Tanker Crashes

Age of Driver	Number of Fatal Crashes
Under 20	3
20-29	10
30-39	6
40-49	4
50-59	4
60-69	4
70 and over	2
Unknown	5

TABLE 2-3
Gender of Firefighters Fatally Injured in Tanker Crashes

Gender	Number of Deceased
Male	37
Female	5
Total	42

TABLE 2-5
States in Which Fatal Tanker Crashes Occurred

State	Number of Fatal Crashes
Texas	6
California	3
Virginia	3
Kentucky	3
Tennessee	3
Mississippi	3
Pennsylvania	3
Arkansas	2
Louisiana	2
Missouri	2
Alabama	1
Indiana	1
Michigan	1
North Carolina	1
Oregon	1
South Carolina	1
Washington	1
West Virginia	1

TIME OF DAY

A review of the reported times of day that the crashes occurred shows that most tanker accidents occur during daylight hours **(Table 2-6)**. The most common three-hour time frame in which tanker crashes occurred was the noon to 3 p.m. period. That time period accounted for 32 percent of all fatal tanker crashes. When one combines that time period with the 3 p.m. to 6 p.m. period, 55 percent of all tanker crashes occurred during the afternoon. This is despite the fact that historically USFA and NFPA annual fire loss reports show that the greatest percentage of working fires occur at night.

TABLE 2-6 Time of Day When Crashes Occur	
Time of Day	Number of Fatal Crashes
Midnight to 2:59 am	1
3 a.m. to 5:59 a.m.	3
6 a.m. to 8:59 a.m.	0
9 a.m. to 11:59 a.m.	2
Noon to 2:59 p.m.	12
3 p.m. to 5:59 p.m.	9
6 p.m. to 8:59 p.m.	4
9 p.m. to 11:59 p.m.	5
Not Reported	2

The statistical significance of this information is not totally clear. One possibility is that drivers are more confident when driving in daylight than in dark. This confidence may translate into greater speed or overconfidence in one's driving ability. Both of those factors have historically been shown to be significant causes of emergency vehicle crashes. The reduced visibility that occurs during nighttime driving may actually save lives, as it forces the driver to slow down. Other causal factors that may be responsible for more daytime collisions include more civilian vehicles on the road during this time of the day and the greater use of mutual and automatic aid in many jurisdictions on daytime responses.

CAUSAL FACTORS FOR TANKER CRASHES

The case history information that was available for the 38 incidents that were studied did contain extensive information on the various causes and factors that led to the crashes. In virtually every case, there was more than one cause or factor listed as having played a significant role in the occurrence or the seriousness of the crash. **Table 2-7** shows a compilation of the contributing causes for the 38 cases that were studied.

Failure to wear a seatbelt was noted in 31 of the 42 fatalities. While failure to wear a seatbelt is rarely the *cause* of a crash, it often plays a significant role in the severity of injury to the victims. Nearly three-quarters (actually 73.8 percent) of the firefighters killed in tanker crashes were not wearing seatbelts. While there is no conclusive manner to determine how many of these victims would have been saved had they been wearing their seatbelts, it is a safe assumption that a large majority of them would. This assumption applies especially to the 20 victims who were partially or totally ejected from the apparatus. As stated in Chapter 1, the chances of surviving a crash are many times greater if the victim is confined to the inside of the vehicle.

When one examines the true *causes* of tanker crashes, four major factors become apparent in Table 2.7:

- the apparatus wheels leaving the right side of the road;

- excessive speed;

- overcorrection/oversteering by the driver when attempting to bring right wheels back onto the road surface; and

- Failure to negotiate a curve.

From those four major factors, two pairs of interrelated causes may be discerned. The first is the combination of allowing the apparatus wheels to drift off the right-side of the road and overcorrection or oversteering when trying to bring the wheels back onto the road surface. In nearly two-thirds (65.8 percent) of the crashes that were studied, the apparatus drifted off the right side of the road. Once the right side wheels were off the roadway, in three-quarters (76 percent) of the cases, the crash then occurred as a result of the driver attempting to bring the vehicle back onto the roadway and then losing control. In the remaining cases, the vehicle either rolled over or struck an object (pole, guardrails, bridge rails, etc.)

TABLE 2-7 Contributing Factors in Fatal Crashes	
Contributing Factors in Fatal Crashes	Number of Fatal Crashes
Failure to wear seatbelts	31
Wheels left the right side of the road	25
Excessive speed	21
Fatally injured individuals ejected from the apparatus	20
Overcorrection when attempting to bring right wheels back onto the road surface	19
Failure to negotiate a curve	17
Loss of control while descending a grade	6
Failure to follow posted speed recommendations on a curve	3
Mechanical failure	2
Poor road condition	1
Poor apparatus design	1
Driver inattention	1
Unknown	1
Impairment by prescription medication	1
Failure to stop at an intersection	1

once the wheels were off the right side of the driving surface. Information on how to avoid these types of crashes and safely bring a vehicle back onto the driving surface are covered in Chapter 4 of this report.

The other pair that is typically interrelated is excessive speed and failure to safely negotiate a curve. In most cases, the reason that the curve was not safely negotiated was because the apparatus entered the curve at an unsafe speed. In several of the cases that were studied, it was noted that the apparatus was well above the posted recommended speed for the curve on which the crash occurred. However, excessive speed is not only a problem when trying to negotiate curves. It is often the reason that the right wheels drift off the road surface, that the apparatus is unable to come to a stop at intersections, or that the driver is unable to control the vehicle when a mechanical failure occurs. Simply slowing down and driving the apparatus at a reasonable speed will prevent a significant number of crashes from occurring.

It should be noted that the incident reports used in this document typically did not directly address the road conditions at the time of the crashes. In only one case did they mention that the road was wet at the time of the crash. It must be assumed that, if adverse road conditions were a significant factor in any of the crashes, they would have been mentioned in the report. It can therefore be concluded that most of the crashes occurred on clear, dry, paved roads.

CONCLUSION

As stated above, much useful information can be gained by studying the records of past tanker crashes. Through this study it was learned that most crashes occur in daylight hours, on clear, dry, paved roads. It has been deduced that driver inexperience may play a role in the crashes because of the large number of young drivers who were operating the tankers at the time of the crashes. This confirms the fact that wearing their seatbelts while driving will save a significant number of drivers. Lastly, by slowing the apparatus down during the response and knowing how to react in the event the right-side wheels leave the roadway will prevent a significant number of crashes from occurring. These facts will serve as the foundation for the information on improving tanker safety that is covered in Chapter 4 of this manual.

FIRE DEPARTMENT TANKER CRASH CASE HISTORIES

3

The first two chapters of this report have spent a considerable amount of time and effort to detail the common causes of crashes involving fire department tankers. However, for many people this information is not relevant unless it can be applied to real-life incidents. In this chapter we will examine case histories of fire department tanker crashes over the past decade that have involved fatalities to firefighters onboard the apparatus.

Pertinent case histories have been selected from insurance company records, U.S. Fire Administration (USFA) records, U.S. Department of Justice Public Safety Officers' Benefit (PSOB) data, and a variety of other private and governmental sources to highlight some of the major causes of crashes that have been discussed to this point in the report. These case histories are highlighted to show the reader that these causal factors have previously resulted in a tragic outcome. Providing these case histories is in no way meant to demean or be critical of the individuals and departments involved in these incidents. It is hoped that these departments would want to share this information with the fire service so that other personnel and jurisdictions could avoid suffering the same tragedy.

Only a small selection of case histories is reviewed in this chapter. For a complete compilation of case histories involving fatal fire department tanker crashes since 1990, see **Appendix A.**

TRAVELING AT AN EXCESSIVE SPEED

Date of Incident: April 17, 1995
Time of Incident: 3:34 a.m.
Location of Incident: Castella, California

The Incident:

A 50-year-old female driver lost control of a 1,000-gallon tanker while responding to a barn fire in an unfamiliar location. A 47-year-old male firefighter was also riding in the right-front seat.

After receiving directions from a local citizen at the roadside, the driver made a wrong turn and eventually descended a steep ½-mile hill. At the bottom of the hill, the tanker failed to negotiate a sharp left turn, struck a bridge guardrail, and either went through the guardrail or rolled over the top of it. The tanker fell into a rain-swollen creek below.

After all other fire department units had returned to the station from the dispatched barn fire, the absence of the tanker and two firefighters was noted. Firefighters fanned out to search for the missing tanker. The tanker was found upside down in the creek about 2-½ hours after the original dispatch.

Both firefighters were found deceased inside of the cab of the apparatus; neither had been wearing a seat belt. The cause of death for the passenger was listed as drowning, and the cause of death for the driver was listed as exposure and hypothermia.

Tire marks, not skid marks that would indicate braking, were found at the bottom of the hill. Causal factors cited in the law enforcement traffic crash report and coroner's report included driver inattention, driver unfamiliarity with the road, and excessive speed for the vehicle and road.

RIGHT WHEELS LEAVE ROAD SURFACE/OVERCORRECTION
Date of Incident: January 14, 1995
Time of Incident: 5:20 p.m.
Location of Incident: Salisbury, North Carolina

The Incident:
A 49-year-old male firefighter was the driver of a tanker responding to a report of a smoke odor in a manufactured home. A second firefighter rode as the front-seat passenger in the vehicle.

Members of the first fire apparatus unit to arrive at the manufactured home were told by other firefighters -- who had responded directly to the scene in their personal vehicles -- that there was no emergency. The operator of the first unit informed other responding units by radio to reduce their response mode to nonemergency. Firefighters standing near the truck heard the sound of the tanker's crash at approximately the same time as this transmission was being made.

It was later determined that the right wheels of the tanker left the roadway. The driver steered the truck back onto the pavement, but the rear end of the tanker came around and the apparatus began to slide. The tanker exited the left side of the road, rolled, and collided with a natural gas distribution substation.

A second tanker -- that was following the one that crashed -- alerted other firefighters to the crash. When firefighters arrived on the scene, they found the tanker entangled in the natural gas substation with large amounts of natural gas being released. A hazardous materials response team from a nearby city was called to the scene. Once the team arrived, the two firefighters were removed from the tanker and transported to the hospital. The driver was pronounced dead at the hospital, the firefighter who had been a passenger in the tanker received serious but non-life- threatening injuries. Neither firefighter was wearing a seatbelt.

The cause of death for the driver was listed as multiple blunt force injuries to the head, chest, and abdomen. The law enforcement report on this incident cited excessive speed as a contributing circumstance to the crash.

POOR APPARATUS DESIGN

Date of Incident: November 5, 1997
Time of Incident: 2:25 p.m.
Location of Incident: Danville, Virginia

The Incident:

The 30-year-old male firefighter who was fatally injured was a passenger in a 1,000-gallon tanker that responded to the scene of a mutual aid structure fire. Upon arrival at the scene, the initial driver was ordered to perform other tasks, and the passenger became the driver of the tanker. Water from the tanker was unloaded at the fire scene, and the tanker left to refill at a nearby fire hydrant. A third firefighter accompanied the new driver to the fill site.

After the tanker had been refilled, the tanker headed back to the fire scene. As the apparatus exited a curve, the right wheels left the roadway and ran onto the shoulder. The driver overcorrected to the left, which brought the apparatus briefly into the oncoming lane of traffic. The driver corrected again to the right and the rear of the apparatus began to slide around. The tanker continued to slide and began to roll at some point. The vehicle came to rest on its roof, off of the right side of the road.

Neither firefighter was wearing a seatbelt and both were ejected from the tanker at some point in the rollover. The driver received fatal traumatic injuries, and the other firefighter survived his injuries.

While at first glance this incident involves failure to keep the apparatus on the roadway, the investigation revealed that the water tank was only baffled to prevent forward and backward motion of the load. It did not have baffles to prevent sideward sloshing. It is believed that this accentuated the difficulty in regaining control of the vehicle once it began to slide sideways.

FAILURE TO YIELD RIGHT-OF-WAY

Date of Incident: November 2, 2000
Time of Incident: 2:30 a.m.
Location of Incident: Overisel Township, Michigan

The Incident:

The 41-year-old female firefighter who was fatally injured in this crash was the passenger in a 2,000-gallon tanker responding to a mutual-aid structure fire involving a turkey farm. As the apparatus approached an intersection, a pickup truck approaching the intersection from the other street was thought by the occupants of the tanker to be yielding the right-of-way to the tanker. The tanker may have slowed before going through the stop sign, but it did not come to a complete stop. As the tanker proceeded through the intersection, it was struck by the pickup at the left rear axle.

The force of the impact deflated the right rear tires of the tanker and the apparatus began to swerve from side to side. The tanker left the left side of the roadway, rolled over, and the water tank separated from the chassis

(Figure 3-1). The tanker came to rest upside down with both firefighters trapped in the cab. Neither firefighter was wearing a seatbelt at the time of the crash.

Firefighters from other departments responding to the fire came upon the crash scene and provided aid. Both firefighters were extricated from the cab (Figure 3-2). The passenger was pronounced dead at the scene as a result of crushing blunt force chest injuries; her cause of death was listed as mechanical and positional asphyxiation. The injuries to the tanker driver and the driver of the pickup were not life threatening.

Figure 3-1 The water tank separated from the chassis after the vehicle left the roadway.

Figure 3-2 Occupants required extrication from the crushed cab.

MECHANICAL FAILURE -- TIRE BLOWOUT

Date of Incident: August 19, 2001
Time of Incident: 12:45 p.m.
Jurisdiction of Incident: Odell, Oregon

The Incident:

The 52-year-old male driver was returning to his fire district with a 2,000-gallon tanker that had undergone water tank repairs. The driver was the sole occupant of the tanker. The water tank was empty.

While going down the freeway at a speed estimated at 60 miles per hour, the right front tire of the tanker experienced a blowout. The tanker veered to the right, crossed the shoulder, and went into a level field of grass and rocks. The tanker traveled at an angle through the field for about 300 feet before striking a number of large boulders and a tree.

The cab of the tanker was severely damaged and the driver -- who was not wearing a seatbelt -- was trapped in the vehicle. Responding firefighters removed the driver from the tanker, however he was pronounced dead at the scene. The cause of death was listed as blunt force trauma to the head, abdomen, and upper and lower extremities.

MECHANICAL FAILURE -- BRAKE SYSTEM FAILURE
Date of Incident: May 25, 1997
Time of Incident: 1:22 p.m.
Location of Incident: Jacksboro, Tennessee

The Incident:

The 41-year-old male firefighter who was fatally injured was the right-front-seat passenger in a tanker that was responding to a crash with fire on a local highway. Neither the driver nor the passenger was wearing a seatbelt at the time of the crash.

As the apparatus approached an intersection, the driver attempted to slow the vehicle but the brakes failed. The tanker proceeded through the intersection at a speed later estimated to be 30 miles per hour.

On the other side of the intersection, in the tanker's path, a child was playing in the road. In order to avoid hitting the child, the driver was forced to swerve left. The tanker exited the left side of the roadway and began to roll onto its right side after coming into contact with a power pole guide wire. The tanker then slid and rolled to the other side of the roadway, struck another power pole, and came to rest on its roof. The passenger was ejected when the tanker collided with the guide wire. The tanker crushed the firefighter's head as it rolled.

An inspection of the tanker's braking system after the crash found a hole in a brake line near the rear axle differential.

POOR ROAD CONDITIONS
Date of Incident: May 12, 1995
Time of Incident: 2:40 p.m.
Location of Incident: Jacksonville, Arkansas

The Incident:

The 22-year-old female firefighter who was fatally injured was the right-front-seat passenger in a 1,000-gallon tanker that was engaged in driver training. Both the driver and firefighter were wearing lap-type seatbelts.

Figure 3-3 Note the cracks in the asphalt at the road's edge.

As the tanker proceeded on a small local road, the asphalt on the right side of the road crumbled **(Figure 3-3)**. The driver of the tanker oversteered in an attempt to recover control, the apparatus left the roadway on the left side of the road, and it struck a driveway culvert. The apparatus vaulted slightly and began to rotate. The vehicle rolled and came to rest upside down, partially in the roadway **(Figure 3-4)**.

The passenger received fatal traumatic injuries; the driver of the apparatus was injured but his injuries were not life threatening.

Figure 3-4 The vehicle came to rest on the opposite side of the road.

FAILURE TO FOLLOW POSTED SPEED SUGGESTIONS ON A CURVE

Date of Incident: April 8, 1996
Time of Incident: 9:36 p.m.
Location of Incident: Moses Lake, Washington

The Incident:

The 19-year-old male firefighter who was fatally injured was the driver of a 3,000-gallon tanker responding to a structure fire. The right-front seat was occupied by another firefighter. Neither firefighter was wearing a seatbelt at the time of the crash.

A local bridge was out of service for repair so the response route taken to the fire was unfamiliar to both firefighters. The fire chief, who was following the tanker in his vehicle, was more familiar with the route. As the tanker approached a curve, the fire chief realized that the driver was accelerating and ordered the tanker, by radio, to slow down. The order came too late and the tanker entered the curve at a speed estimated to be 40 to 60 miles per hour. The recommended speed in the curve is 35 miles per hour.

The tanker skidded, rotated counterclockwise, and then left the right side of the roadway. The tanker rolled first onto its right side, then onto its roof. The cab was crushed as it slid for a distance. The tanker rolled again and came to rest on its left side.

The fire chief and another chief officer who was riding with him immediately requested assistance. They found the passenger attempting to self-extricate and helped him out of the vehicle. They had a great deal of difficulty removing the driver due to his position in the cab of the truck. He was eventually removed with the assistance of a passing motorist. CPR was begun immediately and continued while the driver was transported to the hospital. The driver was pronounced dead shortly after his arrival at the hospital. The cause of death for the driver was listed as a lacerated heart and major vessels.

CONCLUSION

The first two chapters of this publication focused on generalized data and statistics regarding fatal fire department tanker crashes. While that information is highly useful in allowing us to understand the overall problem better, it is a review of case studies that "personalizes" these crashes. By looking at the circumstances surrounding individual crashes, it is often possible to put oneself in the position of the tanker driver or relate to the conditions that faced the unfortunate driver in the case study. This, in turn, will allow current and future tanker drivers to more easily recognize more easily the causes of crashes and avoid them in the future.

PREVENTING FIRE DEPARTMENT TANKER CRASHES

4

The preceding chapters in this manual have covered the causes of fire department tanker crashes, statistical information on their frequency and severity, and pertinent case studies to highlight the problem. While all of this information is interesting, it is not particularly useful unless it is used to construct a plan of action directed at reducing the frequency and severity of these events. To paraphrase a popular old saying: those who fail to recognize and deal with their past may be doomed to repeat it.

It is the goal of this document to recognize the problems associated with tanker crashes that have occurred in the past and to provide strategies for their avoidance in the future. Using the information provided to this point in this manual as a basis, this chapter is intended to provide fire department personnel with information that can be applied directly toward developing programs, procedures, and strategies that lead to safer operation of fire department tankers. Information covered in this chapter includes driver training, apparatus maintenance programs, apparatus design issues, proper driving techniques, and onscene operations.

DRIVER TRAINING PROGRAMS

Any fire department, whether career, volunteer, or industrial, must have an established and thorough training program for prospective fire apparatus drivers, including those who will be required/allowed to drive tankers. Simply letting a firefighter drive the tanker around the block a few times and showing him or her how to engage the fire pump or operate the tank dump valve is not adequate. An effective training program consists of appropriate amounts of classroom (theoretical) instruction, practical training in the field (application), and testing to ensure that the person is ready for the responsibility in a real-world setting. In this section of the chapter, we will examine the important elements of a training program for prospective drivers of fire department tankers.

Applicable NFPA Standards

Before getting into any detailed discussion on fire department tanker driver training, it is necessary to recognize the two primary National Fire Protection Association (NFPA) standards that relate directly to this issue. These standards are only considered "the law" if they have been formally adopted by some authority having jurisdiction. However, their status as nationally recognized, consensus-developed documents has historically been upheld in civil legal proceedings in all levels of the court system. Thus, there is an impetus on fire departments and training organizations to follow these standards in order to avoid being subjected to civil liability in the event of a lawsuit.

NFPA 1002

NFPA 1002, *Standard for Fire Apparatus Driver/Operator Professional Qualifications,* establishes the minimum job performance requirements for personnel who drive and operate fire apparatus. This standard covers a wide array of fire department vehicles, including tankers. Drivers are not necessarily expected to meet the entire standard. Rather, drivers are only required to meet those portions of the standard that apply to the particular type of apparatus they will be expected to drive.

In the case of personnel being trained to drive fire department tankers, at a minimum these personnel must meet the requirements contained in the following chapters of NFPA 1002:

- Chapter 1: Administration -- This chapter contains mostly information on procedural issues for administration of the standard. The only two substantive requirements contained in this chapter are that the candidate be appropriately licensed according to State or Provincial motor vehicle codes and that they meet the medical requirements contained in NFPA 1582, *Standard on Medical Requirements for Fire Fighters and Information for Fire Department Physicians.*

- Chapter 2: General Requirements -- This chapter contains requirements for performing and documenting routine vehicle maintenance functions, for driving the vehicle under a variety of conditions, and for being able to operate any fixed equipment (generators, floodlights, etc.) that is on the vehicle.

- Chapter 8: Mobile Water Supply Apparatus -- This chapter contains requirements for performing and documenting routine vehicle maintenance functions specific to tankers and for being able to establish and operate water shuttle fill site and dump site operations.

If the tanker that the driver will operate is equipped with a fire pump, the candidate also must meet the requirements contained in Chapter 3, *Apparatus Equipped With an Attack or Fire Pump.* This chapter contains requirements for maintaining pump components, pumping supply and attack lines, and operating the pump from a pressurized or static water supply source. It should be noted that both Chapters 3 and 8 of NFPA 1002 require that the candidate also be certified as a Fire Fighter I in accordance with NFPA 1001, *Standard for Fire Fighter Professional Qualifications,* before being certified to NFPA 1002 to drive a tanker.

NFPA 1451

NFPA 1451, *Standard for a Fire Service Vehicle Operations Training Program,* provides direction to fire departments on establishing and maintaining emergency vehicle driver training programs. This standard requires departments to have a fully documented training program for anyone who will be allowed or required to drive fire department vehicles, including tankers. According to NFPA 1451, the driver training program should include the following elements:

- general rules and considerations;
- training and education requirements, including information on training frequency, instructor qualifications, and training program safety;

- information on applicable laws and liabilities;
- detailed information on departmental procedures for emergency response situations;
- crash and injury prevention measures;
- crash review and documentation procedures; and
- vehicle and apparatus care procedures.

It is strongly recommended that any fire department developing a driver training program consult this standard and follow it as much as possible. The remainder of this section highlights, in detail, the important components of the driver training program.

Components of the Driver Training Program

Establishing an effective fire apparatus or tanker driver training program is not a quick and simple process. There are multiple components of a properly designed driver training program, including both classroom (theoretical) and practical (hands-on) training sessions. In order to bring all of these elements together into an effective training program, considerable planning, organization, and preparation will be required. This section highlights some of the more important aspects that must be considered when putting together a training program for personnel who will be expected to drive tankers, or for that matter any other fire apparatus.

TRAINING FREQUENCY

One of the first issues that must be considered in developing a driver training program is determining when personnel must be put into the program and what the frequency of continuing training should be. According to NFPA 1451, drivers must receive training as follows:

- before being certified to become a fire apparatus driver;
- not less than twice per year after being certified as a driver;
- anytime the apparatus they drive has undergone significant mechanical changes; and
- anytime the driver operator will be expected to drive a new or unfamiliar vehicle.

The first bullet point above seems very obvious. As has been stated previously in this document, no firefighter should ever drive a fire apparatus on a public thoroughfare unless he or she has been previously trained and certified to do so. When the firefighter receives the training to become a driver depends on local fire department protocols. Some fire departments include fire apparatus driver training as part of their basic recruit training. These firefighters become qualified fire apparatus drivers from the very beginning of their career on the fire department. Other fire departments require firefighters to gain one or more years of experience as a firefighter before being qualified to enter into the driver training program. Whatever the case, remember that if your fire department wishes to meet the intent of the NFPA 1002 standard, the candidates will also have to have their Fire Fighter I certification per NFPA 1001 prior to being able to certify as a fire apparatus driver.

NFPA 1451 also specifies that all qualified fire apparatus drivers complete as least two continuing education driver training classes per year following their initial training and certification. These classes are necessary to ensure that the drivers' skills have not deteriorated, that they have not picked up any bad habits since their initial training, and to update them on changes in technology or departmental procedures that affect their driving chores. At least part of this training must include on-the-road driving exercises. Operating in a driving simulator, while an effective learning tool, is not considered a suitable substitute for actual driving time.

If the apparatus that the driver has been previously trained to drive undergoes some type of major change or renovation, the driver should be retrained on these aspects of apparatus operation before being allowed to drive the apparatus again under live conditions. For example, if the tanker was previously equipped with a gasoline engine and a manual shift transmission but has under gone a rehabilitation that included the installation of a diesel engine and automatic transmission, the driver should be retrained on that apparatus.

Lastly, it goes almost without saying that if a previously certified driver's station is assigned a new vehicle, or the driver is assigned to a new station with vehicles that are unlike those he or she was trained on and accustomed to driving, proper training on the new vehicle must be completed before the driver is allowed to operate the vehicle in the field.

INSTRUCTOR QUALIFICATIONS

The fire department must ensure that only qualified personnel are allowed to serve as instructors for driver training programs. It is recommended that all instructors be certified at least to the Instructor I level contained in NFPA 1041, *Standard for Fire Service Instructor Professional Qualifications*. The instructors themselves should also be qualified drivers of the apparatus being used for training. Instructors that will be teaching fire department tanker operations should also be familiar with water shuttle operations, in addition to vehicle operation, so that safe operating principles for these operations can be incorporated into the training program (**Figure 4-1**).

Figure 4-1 Tanker driving instructors must be familiar with water shuttle operations.

CLASSROOM (THEORETICAL) INSTRUCTION

In recent years, there have been those in the fire service training field who have advocated the reduction or elimination of classroom or theoretical instruction. The theory behind this philosophy is that available training time is limited and that most of the skills a firefighter requires are physical tasks. Though this training philosophy has been successfully implemented in some jurisdictions, the majority of the fire service still recognizes the value of classroom instruction as an important part of the overall training of prospective fire apparatus drivers. Providing personnel with the theory and background information on driving fire apparatus will better prepare them to get behind the wheel of the apparatus and begin training on the physical tasks of operating a fire department tanker. At a minimum, classroom instruction for prospective tanker drivers should include

- applicable laws and liabilities;
- departmental policies and standard operating procedures (SOP's);
- vehicle dynamics;
- emergency and nonemergency driving procedures;
- crash and injury prevention measures; and
- Vehicle and apparatus care procedures.

Applicable laws and liabilities. This portion of the class should include a thorough review of all of the local, State, and Federal laws and regulations that apply to emergency vehicle drivers. The candidates must receive specific instruction on regulations and departmental policies that allow emergency vehicles to disregard specific regulations, such as speed limits, passing through stop signals, and crossing the centerline of the roadway. All fire departments must have written copies of policies that allow for these waivers. The candidates should also be informed of the conditions and limitations of their personal and civil liability and the degree to which the fire department provides such protection for them. The candidates should also be informed of any licensing requirements they need to meet in order to drive fire apparatus. Some States require fire apparatus operators to obtain a commercial driver's license (CDL) and others do not. Fire departments located in States that have exempted fire apparatus drivers from CDL requirements may wish to consider a departmental policy that requires obtaining such a license. This extra step will help to ensure the competence of the driver and provides an extra measure against liability issues should the driver ever be involved in a crash.

Departmental policies and SOP's. Drivers cannot be expected to follow departmental policies and SOP's unless they know what they are. Any training program should include a thorough review of this information. Deviations from applicable local, State, or Federal laws should be highlighted in particular. All departments should be able to provide their members with written copies of these procedures, usually in the form of an SOP manual or similar document. The classroom training program should assist the students in becoming familiar with searching for and interpreting the pertinent regulations for tanker operations that are contained in these documents.

Vehicle dynamics. Theoretical instruction should include basic information on the physical dynamics of fire department tankers and their operations. This knowledge can then be applied to actual driving situations when the practical, hands-on portion of the training program is reached. Some of the vehicle dynamics issues that are of particular importance in tanker driver training programs include

- The relationship of weight and speed to the stopping distance of the vehicle -- Tankers are heavier than most other types of apparatus, and it should be expected that it will take a greater distance to bring them to a complete stop than it would for a smaller vehicle traveling at the same speed. It also goes without saying that the faster the vehicle is going, the more distance it will take to bring it to a complete stop. The driver must be familiar with the stopping characteristics of the tanker in order to ensure that appropriate following distances are used when driving the tanker.

- The extreme weight difference between driving a tanker with a full water tank and an empty tank -- Each 1,000 gallons of water carried on a tanker weighs approximately 4 tons. Thus, a 3,000 gallon tanker weighs 12 tons more when it is traveling to a fire scene than it does after it dumps its load and heads for more water at a fill site. The vehicle handles significantly different when it is empty than when it is full. For example, the empty tanker will be more likely to skid on a wet road surface than would a full tanker. No other type of apparatus is subject to more drastic amounts of weight differences during normal operations.

- The effects of a partially full water tank on vehicle handling -- Driving tankers can be most dangerous when the water tank is only partially filled. This danger is magnified if the tank is not properly baffled. The effects of water sloshing back and forth within the tank, often referred to as *liquid surge*, can overwhelm the driver's ability to handle the vehicle. For example, when the driver applies the brakes in a harsh manner to attempt a quick stop, the water in the tank will surge to the front of the tank and create additional momentum. This added momentum could override the braking system's ability to stop the vehicle and push it further forward. If the tank is not properly baffled according to requirement of NFPA 1901, *Standard for Automotive Fire Apparatus*, it should be driven only when the tank is completely full or completely empty.

- The effects of a high center of gravity -- Tankers tend not only to be heavier than most other fire vehicles, they also tend to have a higher center of gravity. This can be a particular problem when attempting to negotiate severe curves or sharp turns at high rates of speed. Momentum could cause the tanker to leave the roadway or roll over **(Figure 4-2)**. The driver should be instructed about these dangers and how to avoid them when they are driving the vehicle. The best way to avoid them is to slow down and drive the vehicle at a safe speed. The safe speed will vary for each vehicle depending on its size and design. The driver needs to find out the handling characteristics of the tanker he or she will be driving, and learn the appropriate speeds at which curves and turns may be negotiated.

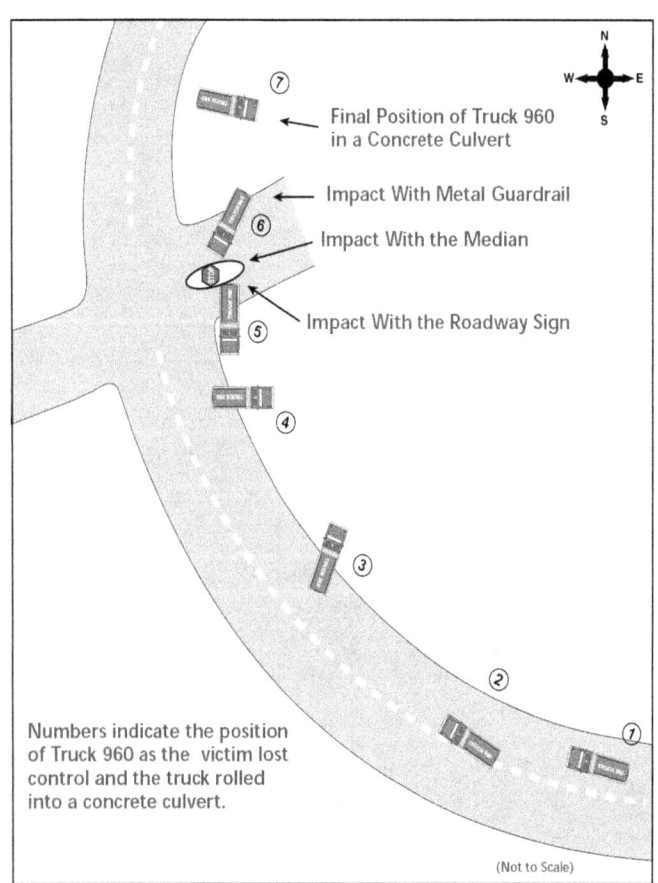

Final Position of Truck 960 in a Concrete Culvert

Impact With Metal Guardrail

Impact With the Median

Impact With the Roadway Sign

Numbers indicate the position of Truck 960 as the victim lost control and the truck rolled into a concrete culvert.

(Not to Scale)

Figure 4-2 Momentum may cause the tanker to leave the roadway. *Courtesy of NIOSH*

SAFE OPERATION OF FIRE TANKERS

Emergency and nonemergency driving procedures. The classroom training session should provide an overview of the proper procedures that should be followed when driving the tanker during emergency responses and nonemergency conditions. Some of this information may already have been covered during the portion of the lesson that covered departmental policies and SOP's. However, this portion of the class also should reinforce common driving techniques and safety procedures that may not be contained in the departmental SOP's. Issues that should be reviewed include

- Situations that demand the vehicle be brought to a complete stop and when it is safe to proceed. These situations include posted stop signs, red traffic signals, activated railroad crossings, blind intersections, and intersections where right-of-way for all lanes of traffic cannot be determined **(Figure 4-3)**.

- Requirements related to encountering stopped school buses with activated warning flashers. Most States require apparatus to come to a complete stop in these situations unless the apparatus is traveling in the opposite direction on a divided roadway.

Figure 4-3 Be extremely cautious when approaching railroad crossings that are protected only by passive warning signs.

- Safe following distances behind other fire apparatus or civilian vehicles.

- Overtaking and passing other vehicles during an emergency response.

- Predetermined response routes used in that jurisdiction.

More detailed information on addressing each of these situations is contained later in this chapter.

Crash and injury prevention measures. The classroom training session should include information on crash and injury prevention that has been gleaned from both local and fire service-wide experiences. By addressing common hazards that are encountered by fire-service personnel -- in particular apparatus drivers -- and the mitigation of these hazards, a significant reduction in the frequency and severity of accidents can be realized. Some of the information that should be included in this portion of the program includes

- Risk identification and correction procedures used by your fire department.

- Avoiding operating vehicles in reverse whenever practically possible.

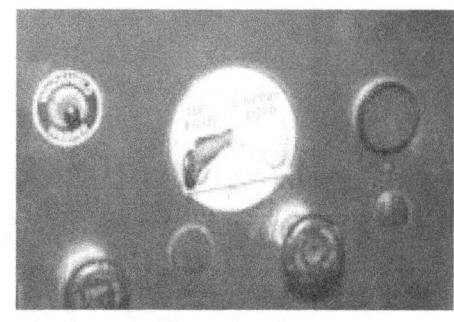

- Operating vehicles equipped with manual brake limiting valves, often referred to as wet/dry road switches, with the valve in the "dry road" position at all times **(Figure 4-4)**. Federal law now requires these switches to be disconnected in the dry road position.

- Proper apparatus positioning techniques that provide a barrier between firefighters and oncoming traffic.

Figure 4-4 Wet/Dry road switches should be left in the dry road position at all times.

- Safe procedures for riding apparatus, including wearing seatbelts, wearing head and eye protection when riding in open seating areas, and hearing protection in riding positions that exceed 90 decibels (dBa).
- Safe methods for loading firehose onto a moving apparatus.

Again, details on these procedures are contained later in this chapter. If available, State Police accident reconstruction or highway enforcement personnel may be invited to present case study information on previous crashes. This type of firsthand information is very effective in implanting the importance of safe and responsible vehicle operation in the prospective driver's mind.

Apparatus care procedures. The classroom portion of the training class should provide the driver with information on the department's procedures for vehicle care and maintenance. The driver's role in inspecting the apparatus and correcting minor deficiencies should be explained. Procedures for reporting significant defects and conditions when the apparatus should be removed from service should also be highlighted.

PRACTICAL DRIVING TRAINING AND EVALUATION

While providing prospective fire apparatus drivers with a solid theoretical background on the requirements of the job is very important, the most important part of the candidate training program, from a safety prospective, is the practical driving portion of the program. It is during this portion of the program that the candidates will learn and develop the skills necessary to safely operate the apparatus in emergency and nonemergency response situations.

The practical driving portion of the program should be progressive in nature. That is, the drivers begin with basic vehicle familiarization tasks. The next step might then be completing simple tasks or maneuvers at slow speeds in a very controlled atmosphere. After they have mastered the simpler skills, they may then progress to more complicated procedures and over-the-road driving. By using this approach, the candidates will become increasingly familiar and comfortable with the handling characteristics of the vehicle before they will be expected to operate it in a more challenging environment.

It is very important that the vehicles used during the training program be the same or very similar to those that the driver will be expected to operate when he or she completes training and is released into the field. This is particularly true when preparing drivers to drive fire department tankers because of their large size and unique handling characteristics. Simply stated, a driver candidate who completes a training program while operating a minipumper or standard fire department pumper will not be safely prepared to drive a 3,000-gallon tanker once he or she is in the field. If the drivers will be expected to drive the large tanker in the field, they should complete all portions of the practical training program using that tanker or one that is similar.

It is also important that the training program include preparing the driver to operate under special conditions that may be particular to that jurisdiction. This may include conditions such as wet or icy roadways, unpaved roadways, and driving on severe grades.

Training safety. Every effort must be made to ensure that the practical training program is conducted in as safe a manner as possible. Remember, you are dealing with candidates who previously may have never driven anything larger than a pickup truck. Making the transition to a large fire department tanker will be a dramatic one for most candidates. By following basic safety procedures and common sense, we can ensure that their learning experience is a safe and effective one. Some of the basic safety procedures that should be followed during practical driver training include

- Training administrators and organizational safety officers must review the training program and lesson plans to ensure that they comply with departmental policies and safety procedures.

- Training officials and safety officers should inspect the training course prior to the commencement of training exercises to make sure that the training area is in proper repair and all appropriate safety equipment is in place.

- A safety officer should be designated during training exercises, and he or she must have the authority to stop all activities and apparatus movement when he or she notices a condition or event that poses the imminent threat of crash or injury.

- All candidates should be under the direct supervision of a qualified driving instructor at all times when operating vehicles on the training ground.

- Designated areas should be cordoned off for conducting driving exercises. No other vehicular traffic should be allowed in the training area while candidates are operating vehicles.

- If multiple vehicles are being used for training at the same time, the training agency should have procedures in place to ensure that the vehicles stay a safe distance apart during the exercise.

- All instructors and candidates should be instructed in hand and radio signals that may be used during the training exercise and the actions that should be taken when particular signals are given.

Driving course exercises. The driver's initial opportunities to get behind the wheel of the apparatus and drive it should be limited to exercises that are conducted in a strictly controlled environment. The common term for this controlled environment is a driving course. Some jurisdictions are fortunate to have a specially designed driving course as part of their training facilities **(Figure 4-5)**. These driving courses may be either a grid or circuit of roadways that simulate public thoroughfares, a large paved driving pad on which various driving courses may be laid out, or a combination of both.

Figure 4-5 Many training academies have specially designed apparatus driver training courses.

Most jurisdictions are not fortunate enough to have this type of driving course on their own property. In these cases the fire department needs to arrange with a property owner in its jurisdiction to use their driveways or parking lots for these exercises. Suitable facilities may be found at schools, churches, sports facilities, shopping centers or malls, and industrial plants. The fire department should obtain permission from the property owner prior to conducting these exercises, and it should also make sure that the area used for training can be segregated from any other vehicular or pedestrian traffic or activities that may be taking place at the facility.

Prior to conducting driving exercises on acquired facilities, the training officer should ensure that the composition of the driving surface is substantial enough to support the weight of heavy fire apparatus. Some parking lots and driveways are not constructed to the same specifications as public thoroughfares. If the driving surface is not substantial enough to handle the weight of a maneuvering tanker, significant damage could be done to the property. The potential for this danger is magnified on asphalt surfaces during periods of extremely hot weather. The asphalt will become soft and the tires of the apparatus will create ruts in the driving surface.

The practical driving exercises may start with a variety of simple procedures. The drivers may be allowed to drive around the course at a slow speed so that they can begin to build confidence in their ability to handle the vehicle. Making the drivers stop at various intervals will allow them to begin becoming familiar with the braking characteristics of the vehicle. Over time they may be allowed to operate the vehicle at increasingly higher speeds so that they begin to develop vehicle handling skills at the speeds that they will be expected to operate when they are in the public.

In addition to simply driving the vehicle around the training area, there are a variety of obstacle and training courses that may be laid out using traffic cones that will increase the drivers' ability to maneuver the vehicle skillfully. These exercises are designed to simulate conditions that the drivers will commonly encounter in the performance of their duties. There are literally dozens of different courses that can be set up. Many are based on specific conditions that are found within the response district of that particular jurisdiction. However, at a minimum, it is recommended that the driver be required to successfully master the four exercises that are required for certification under NFPA 1002. These exercises are

- The Alley Dock Exercise: This exercise measures the driver's ability to pull past a simulated dock or stall, back into the space provided, and stop smoothly. Real-life situations that this exercise simulate include backing the apparatus down an alley or backing the apparatus into its fire station bay **(Figure 4-6)**.

- The Serpentine Exercise: This exercise measures a driver's ability to steer the apparatus forward and backward around fixed objects, within close limits, without stopping. It simulates moving around parked vehicles or other objects at a fire scene **(Figure 4-7)**.

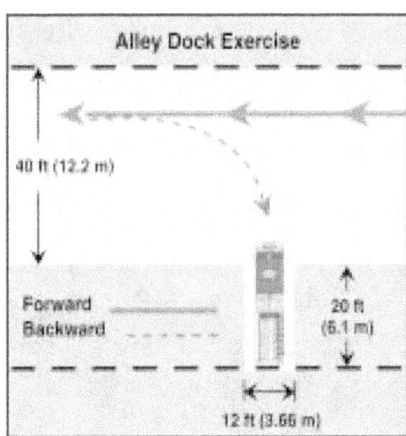

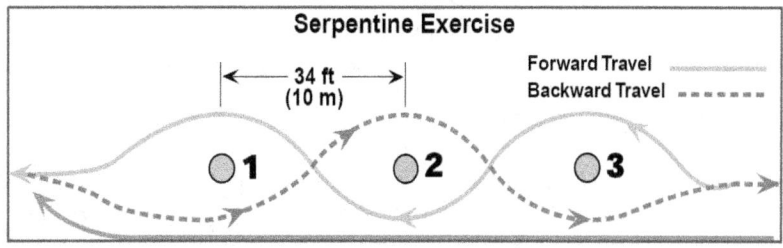

Figure 4-6 The Alley Dock Exercise. *Courtesy of IFSTA/Fire Protection Publications*

Figure 4-7 The Serpentine Exercise. *Courtesy of IFSTA/Fire Protection Publications*

- The Confined Space Turnaround Exercise: This exercise measures the driver's ability to turn the vehicle around in a confined space without striking any objects. This maneuver is often required when the apparatus approaches a congested fire scene and then is ordered to reverse lay a supply line from a pumper on the scene to a water supply source **(Figure 4-8)**.

- The Diminishing Clearance Exercise: This exercise measures the driver's ability to steer the apparatus in a straight line, to judge distances from the vehicle's wheels to fixed objects, and to stop at a finish line. For tanker drivers, this exercise is particularly useful in preparing to approach a water shuttle dump site and prepare to off load water through a side-mounted discharge chute **(Figure 4-9)**.

For more specific directions on constructing these courses and the dimensions that should be used, consult NFPA 1002 or the IFSTA *Pumping Apparatus Driver/Operator Handbook* for directions.

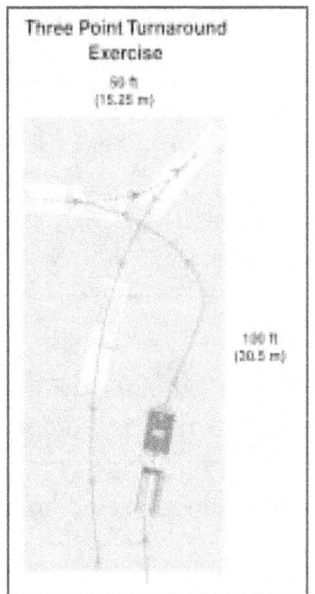

To meet the intent of NFPA 1002, these exercises may be laid out separately and conducted one at a time. However, it is perfectly acceptable to combine two or more of them into a single exercise that requires the driver to accomplish multiple tasks. For example, the nationally recognized *Emer-*

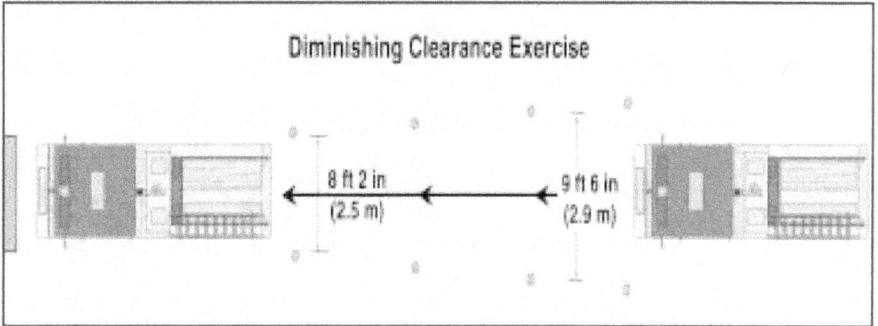

Figure 4-8 The Confined Space Turnaround Exercise. *Courtesy of IFSTA/Fire Protection Publications*

Figure 4-9 The Diminishing Clearance Exercise. *Courtesy of IFSTA/Fire Protection Publications*

gency Vehicle Driver Training Program produced by Volunteer Fireman's Insurance Services (VFIS) contains directions on setting up a single driving course that incorporates all of these exercises into one **(Figure 4-10)**.

Over-the road-training. Once it has been determined that the driver candidate has sufficiently mastered the basics of handling the fire department tanker, the next progression in the training program should be to begin allowing the candidate to operate the vehicle in live traffic situations on public roadways. It is recommended that the candidates first successfully demonstrate their ability to perform all of the required maneuvers on the driving course before they are allowed to begin over-the-road training. As well, consult departmental policies and State motor vehicles codes to determine whether it will be necessary for the driver to obtain a CDL before operating a fire department tanker on a public thoroughfare. It is recommended that a certified driving instructor accompany the candidate at all times when performing over-the-road driver training.

As with the driving course exercises, it is recommended that the driver begin his or her over-the-road driver training by operating the vehicle over a simple route that contains minimal hazards and light civilian traffic. As the driver becomes more comfortable with handling the vehicle in public, an increasingly challenging route may be taken. Before the end of the training program, the driver should be expected to operate the tanker on the most challenging routes within the jurisdiction. If at any time the driver becomes uncomfortable with a situation or shows signs of losing control of the vehicle, the instructor should order the driver to stop the vehicle immediately, but safely.

Each jurisdiction should map out suitable driving courses within its response district. The hazards and challenges presented along these courses may vary. However, it is recommended that various routes include the minimum elements required for certification according to the NFPA 1002 standard. Most CDL testing programs also use a similar list of conditions through which the driver must show the ability to safely operate the vehicle. These elements include

- four left and four right turns;
- a straight section of urban business street or two-lane rural road at least 1 mile long;
- one through intersection and at least two intersections where a stop must be made;
- one railroad crossing;
- one curve, either left or right;
- a section of limited access highway that includes conventional entrance and exit ramps and a section of roadway long enough to make two proper lane changes;
- a downgrade steep and long enough to require downshifting and braking;
- an upgrade steep enough to require gear changing to maintain speed; and
- one underpass or low clearance bridge.

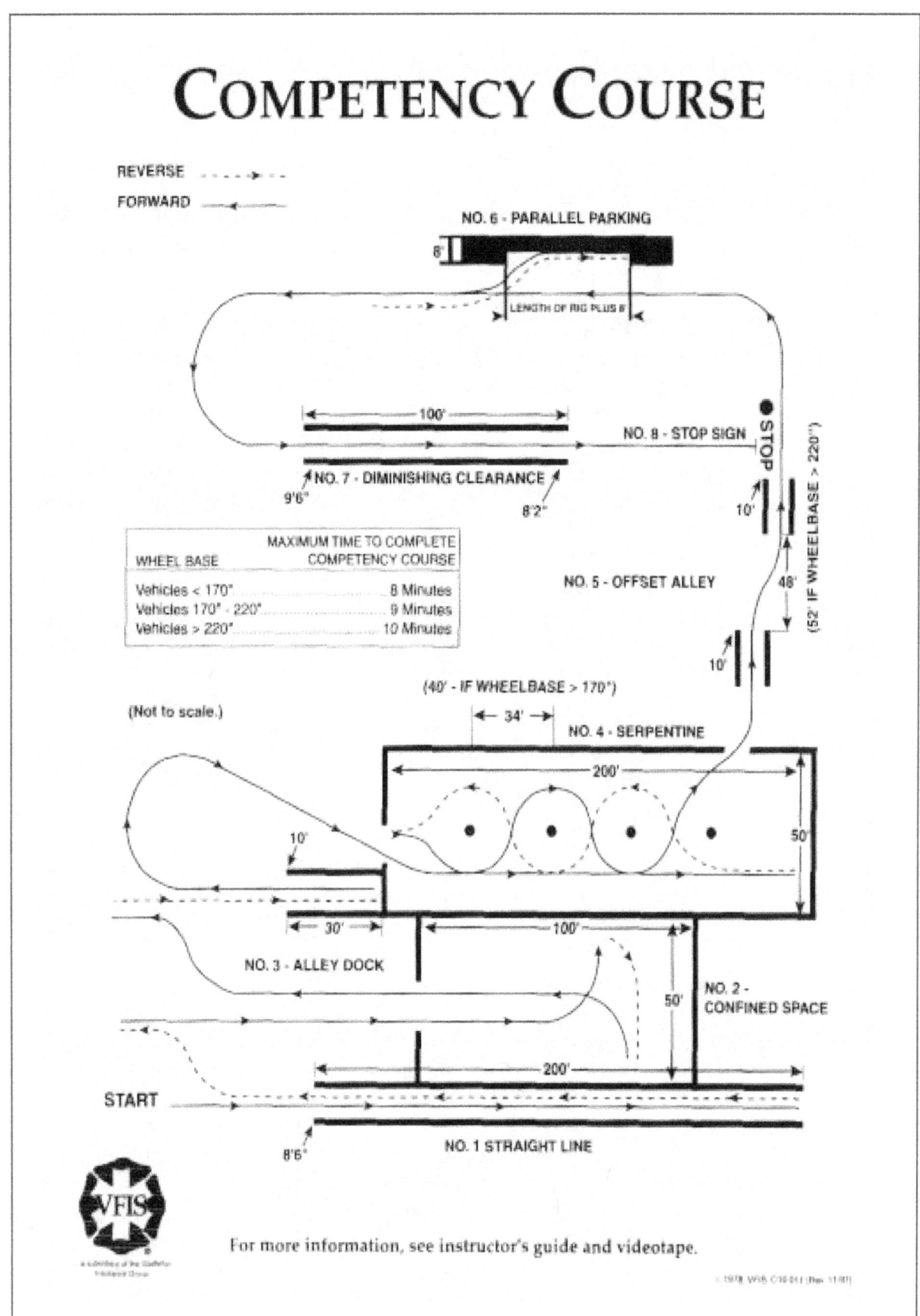

Figure 4-10 The VFIS driving course is used for training in many jurisdictions. *Courtesy of VFIS, York, Pennsylvania*

Once the candidate has successfully completed all of the classroom and practical portions of the training program, he or she should be required to complete a final examination prior to being certified to drive the apparatus in the performance of his or her duties. This should include a written test and practical tests that include driving the vehicle; operating the fire pump and any other mechanical equipment on the apparatus; and, in the case of tanker drivers, establishing and operating water shuttle fill and dump sites. It is recommended that either the National Professional Qualifications Board (NPQB) or the International Fire Service Accreditation Congress (IFSAC) accredit the testing and certification programs.

APPARATUS MAINTENANCE PROGRAMS

Fire apparatus must be capable of performing in the manner for which it was designed at a moment's notice. In order to ensure this, certain preventive maintenance functions must be performed on a regular basis. History has shown that performing routine maintenance checks on a regular basis could have prevented most apparatus or equipment failures. Most fire departments require drivers to be able to perform routine maintenance checks and functions. NFPA 1002 also requires the driver to have certain preventive maintenance skills in order to be certified.

Before continuing, it is important to differentiate between the terms maintenance and repair. *Maintenance*, as used here, means keeping apparatus in a state of usefulness or readiness. Apparatus or equipment that is said to be in a good state of repair has probably been well maintained. Preventive maintenance ensures apparatus reliability, reduces the frequency and cost of repairs, and lessens out-of-service time. The purpose of preventive maintenance is to try to eliminate unexpected and catastrophic failures that could be life and/or property threatening.

Repair means to restore or replace that which has become inoperable. In almost all cases, repair functions are carried out by qualified mechanics who meet the requirements of NFPA 1071, *Standard for Emergency Vehicle Technician Professional Qualifications*. **NOTE:** Repair functions are done by a qualified mechanic -- not the driver.

Preventive Maintenance

Every fire department should have SOP's for a systematic apparatus maintenance program. The SOP's should identify who performs certain maintenance functions, when they are to be performed, how problems that are detected are corrected or reported, and how the process is documented. Fire apparatus maintenance programs should meet the requirements set forth in NFPA 1915, *Standard for Fire Apparatus Preventative Maintenance Program*.

The SOP should clearly dictate those items that drivers are responsible for checking and which conditions they are allowed to correct on their own. Most departments allow the driver to correct certain deficiencies such as low fluid levels and burned-out lightbulbs. More detailed repairs need to be made by a certified mechanic. Large fire departments have their own repair shops and mechanics for this purpose. These mechanics may have their own vehicles and be able to come to a fire station or incident scene to perform a repair. Smaller fire departments may have a local automotive/truck repair business that assists them with these functions.

NFPA 1002 requires drivers to be able to perform basic preventive mainte nance functions by inspecting the following portions of the fire department tanker:

- batteries;
- braking system;
- coolant system;
- electrical system;
- fuel system;
- hydraulic fluids;
- oil;
- tires;
- steering system;
- belts;
- tools, appliances, and equipment;
- water tank and extinguishing agent levels;
- pumping system (if so equipped);
- rapid dump system (if so equipped); and
- foam system (if so equipped).

Drivers should be trained to determine the seriousness of any leaking fluids that may be noticed during the inspection. This includes being able to identify exactly what type of fluid is leaking and whether or not the amount that is leaking constitutes a problem. Some apparatus components regularly leak by their very nature or design. The driver must be able to tell the difference between what is normal and what is not. Some guidance on this issue is provided in NFPA 1915. The standard defines leakage as "the escape of fluid from its intended containment, generally at a connection" and categorizes leaks into one of three classifications:

- Class 1 Leakage -- Seepage of fluid, as indicated by wetness or discolora tion, not great enough to form drops.
- Class 2 Leakage -- Leakage of fluid great enough to form drops, but not enough to cause the drops to fall from the item being inspected.
- Class 3 Leakage -- Leakage of fluid great enough to cause drops to fall from the item being inspected.

The fire department must establish, through its SOP's, to what extent the driver is responsible for checking and correcting deficiencies in each of these areas. On critical safety components, such as braking systems, the driver should not attempt to repair the problem. In these cases, the driver should simply report the problem according to departmental procedures and allow a quali fied mechanic to make the repair.

The schedule for performing maintenance functions and checks varies from department to department. Typically, career fire departments require drivers to perform apparatus inspections and maintenance checks at the beginning of each tour of duty. They may also specify that more detailed work be completed on a weekly or monthly basis. Volunteer fire departments should establish a procedure by which all apparatus are inspected and maintained on at least a weekly or biweekly schedule. These inspections may be made by drivers or designated departmental apparatus officers.

All drivers must be trained to use their department's recordkeeping system. Each fire department apparatus and equipment inspection and maintenance SOP should dictate how maintenance and inspection results should be documented and transmitted to the proper person in the fire department administrative system. Written forms or computer programs may be used to record the information. **Appendix D** contains several examples of apparatus inspection forms that may be used. Fire departments should maintain an effective filing system that allows the information on these reports to be reviewed, stored, and retrieved when required.

Apparatus maintenance and inspection records serve many functions. In a warranty claim, these records may be needed to document that the necessary maintenance was performed. In the event of a crash, maintenance records are likely to be scrutinized by the accident investigators. Proper documentation of recurrent repairs can also assist in deciding whether to purchase new apparatus in lieu of continued repairs on an older unit. Lastly, proper recordkeeping is required by the Insurance Services Office (ISO) in order to receive the available credits when a jurisdiction is being evaluated for its fire insurance rating.

Repairs

In general, fire apparatus drivers are not responsible for performing significant repairs to the apparatus. Each fire department must establish a policy for who will perform major repairs. As mentioned above, larger fire departments may have their own repair facilities and mechanics within the control of the fire department. This is an ideal situation. This allows the fire department to hire and/or train mechanics who are qualified to work on all of the special systems that may be contained on a fire apparatus. Contrary to the beliefs of some, all trucks are not created equal. Because a particular individual is a certified diesel mechanic does not mean that he or she is necessarily adequately prepared to perform the full gamut of required maintenance on fire apparatus. Fire apparatus, including tankers, contain complex electrical systems, pumping and foam proportioning systems, rapid water dumping systems, and any number of other special devices that standard mechanics may not be familiar with.

In jurisdictions where fire apparatus repair is performed at a centralized motor vehicle pool repair facility, it is recommended that the facility employ special mechanics who are trained to work on fire apparatus when the need arises. Again, while the drivetrains used on garbage, dump, and fire trucks may all be similar, little else is. Mechanics trained to work on the special systems contained on fire apparatus are an absolute must.

Smaller jurisdictions commonly use privately owned repair facilities and personnel to perform repairs on their fire apparatus. Rarely are these people certified to work on anything other than the drivetrain of the apparatus. If one of the firefighting systems on the truck is in need of a repair, the manufacturer of the apparatus or the particular system (such as the fire pump) should be contacted to determine where the closest suitable repair facility or personnel may be located.

Numerous serious fire apparatus crashes over the years have been attributed to failure to properly repair noted deficiencies. In all cases, any apparatus that has an identified mechanical deficiency should be removed from service and properly repaired as soon as possible. According to NFPA 1915, each jurisdiction must develop a written policy with criteria for when the apparatus is to be taken out of service. The criterion should be based on the requirements set forth in 49 CFR, part 390, "Federal Motor Carrier Safety Regulations," as well as other local, State, and Federal requirements. The apparatus manufacturer also may have direction on when the apparatus should be removed from service. The repairs must be performed so that the apparatus is brought back to a state of readiness as recommended by the manufacturer of the apparatus.

APPARATUS DESIGN

Numerous crash investigations and reports have cited one or more apparatus design elements as (a) factor(s) in the cause of the crash. These are perhaps among the most tragic of all crash causes, because they are also the most easily preventable causes. It is difficult to predict an apparatus driver's behavior or reactions given a certain circumstance. Humans make mistakes and sometimes these mistakes lead to a crash. That fact can only be controlled to a certain extent. However, the design and construction of the apparatus is completely controllable. Fire department administrators and apparatus officers must understand the impact that various design elements have on the safe operation of the apparatus. Apparatus should be specified and constructed with maximum safety in mind. This is particularly crucial with fire department tankers because of their large size and weight.

The following section highlights some information concerning the most important design factors for both new and used fire department tankers. The factors that are covered here are the ones that are most commonly cited as problematic in tanker crash investigations and reports. The final portion of this section contains relevant information on apparatus visibility issues.

New Apparatus

For the purposes of this report, the term *new apparatus* is intended to mean apparatus that has been constructed by a reputable fire apparatus manufacturer and is ready to be placed in service with a fire department. New apparatus must be built to conform to all applicable NFPA standards, DOT requirements, and other State and Federal motor vehicle regulations. All of these standards and regulations are designed with both safety and functionality in mind. Before being placed in service, the apparatus should be required to pass the acceptance tests that are listed in these standards and regulations. It is a good idea to hire an independent, third-party testing firm to perform these tests whenever possible.

NFPA 1901

The standard that most applies to the design and construction of new fire department tankers is NFPA 1901, *Standard for Automotive Fire Apparatus*. NFPA 1901 is a broad standard covering the design and construction of almost all types of fire apparatus, except for aircraft rescue and firefighting (ARFF) vehicles (covered in NFPA 414) and wildland fire apparatus (covered in NFPA 1906). The standard is divided into 24 chapters. Some chapters are pertinent to all types of apparatus and others are pertinent to specific types of apparatus, such as tankers. New fire department tankers are only required to meet the portions of the standard that are pertinent to the equipment that is carried on that apparatus. For example, if the tanker is not equipped with an aerial device, it does not need to address the requirements in Chapter 18, *Aerial Devices*, of the standard.

Within NFPA 1901, Chapter 5, *Mobile Water Supply Apparatus*, contains some of the most basic requirements for the design of new fire department tankers. The following is a summary of the major requirements contained in this chapter

- In order to be considered a fire department tanker, the apparatus must have a water tank with a capacity of at least 1,000 gallons.
- The tanker must have a minimum of 20 cubic feet of compartment storage space.
- All tankers must carry at least the following pieces of equipment:
  — One 6-pound flat- or pick-head axe,
  — One 6-foot or longer pike pole,
  — At least 200 feet of 2½-inch or larger fire hose,
  — Two portable handlights,
  — A portable dry chemical fire extinguisher with a rating of at least 80-B:C,
  — A 2½-gallon or larger portable water fire extinguisher,
  — At least two SCBA and one spare cylinder for each,
  — A first aid kit,
  — Two spanner wrenches and a hydrant wrench,
  — One each double male and double female hose adaptors, at least 2½-inches in diameter, and
  — Two wheel chocks that fit the vehicle's tires properly.

If the tanker is equipped with a fire or transfer pump, the following minimum provisions also apply

- The pump should meet the requirements of either Chapter 14 (Fire Pumps) or Chapter 16 (Transfer Pumps), whichever applies.

- A minimum of 15 feet of soft intake or 20 feet of hard intake hose with an intake strainer of the appropriate diameter for the pump must be carried on the apparatus.

- At least 400 feet of 1½-, 1¾-, or 2-inch firehose and two combination spray nozzles capable of flowing at least 95 gpm.

- One gated swivel intake connection.

- One rubber mallet.

All fire departments should consult NFPA 1901 when developing the specifi cations for a new tanker. The requirements listed in the standard should be followed as closely as possible. In reality, most reputable apparatus manufac turers will be hesitant, if not completely unwilling, to construct an apparatus that does not completely meet the letter or intent of the standard. To do so would expose them (and the fire department) to civil liability should a crash, injury, and/or death occur as a result of the deviation.

BRAKING SYSTEMS

One of the most important mechanical systems related to safe operation of a fire department tanker is the vehicle's braking system. The ability to slow and stop the vehicle safely and efficiently is crucial. Numerous tanker crashes over the years have been attributed to the driver's inability to slow or stop the ve hicle when the need arises. While in some cases this is a result of excessive speed for the given conditions, cases have been cited where a poorly designed, poorly maintained, or otherwise inadequate braking system was the culprit.

When discussing apparatus braking systems, it is important to differentiate between the three different terms or types of braking systems that enter the discussion:

- *Service Brakes* -- The primary brakes that are manually actuated by the driver via the brake pedal and used to slow or stop a moving apparatus.

- *Parking Brakes* -- Brakes that are applied by the driver to prevent the move ment of a parked apparatus.

- *Auxiliary Braking Systems* -- Braking systems, in addition to the service brakes, that are used to assist in slowing the apparatus when the driver removes his or her foot from the throttle pedal.

NFPA 1901 requires new fire apparatus to be equipped with all-wheel, antilock service braking systems, if such systems are available from the manufacturer of that chassis. In today's market virtually all chassis manufacturers, both custom and commercial, offer these systems. Antilock braking systems pre vent the vehicle's wheels from locking up when the brakes are applied harshly or on slippery surfaces. By allowing the wheels to slow, without locking up, the vehicle will not skid, and the driver will be more able to control the path of travel.

NFPA 1901 recommends that all fire apparatus whose gross vehicle weight rating (GVWR) exceeds 25,000 pounds (which almost all tankers do) have air-actuated braking systems. Air brake systems must have quick air buildup capabilities and dual storage tanks. The air braking system must be equipped with an air dryer and automatic moisture ejector to prevent the buildup of water in the system. Water in the system can be a particular problem in freezing temperatures. Frozen moisture can cause the system to fail and make the driver unable to stop the apparatus. The air braking system must also be equipped with a pressure protection valve that prevents the use of all other air-actuated systems, except for the air-powered windshield wiper and steering systems, should the system's air pressure drop below 80 psi.

Whether or not the apparatus is equipped with an automatic moisture ejector or air drying system, it is strongly recommended that the brake system be manually bled of water at least weekly. This will ensure that any water missed by the automatic equipment will be removed from the system. On apparatus not equipped with dryers or ejectors, manually bleeding the brake system is absolutely essential for ensuring that water buildup does not adversely affect the operation of the braking system.

In particular, fire departments must ensure that commercial chassis vehicles that are used for fire department tankers have adequate braking systems **(Figure 4-11)**. Custom fire apparatus are designed for the special needs of the fire service, but commercial truck chassis may not be. Fire apparatus frequently are required to make successive brake applications within a short period of time. The heating of the brake system can result in momentary loss of braking ability, sometimes referred to as "brake fade." Brake fade at a critical time could result in a crash if the need to stop the vehicle is imminent. In some cases, the standard braking system offered with a particular commercial truck chassis is not sufficient to prevent this problem. The fire department should specify a beefed up braking system to ensure that the vehicle can always be safely stopped.

Figure 4-11 Make sure that the commercial chassis has sufficient braking power for use as a tanker.

The standard also specifies a variety of other requirements for service braking systems, including:

- All brakes on the vehicle must operate at the same time when the brake pedal is applied. This includes trailer brakes if the tanker is of the tractor-trailer type.

- The service brakes must be able to bring a fully loaded vehicle traveling 20 miles per hour to a complete stop in a distance not exceeding 35 feet when operating on a level, dry, hard-surfaced road.

NFPA 1901 requires the apparatus parking brake system to be independent of the service braking system. This feature allows the parking brakes to be applied and stop the vehicle should there be a failure of the service brakes. It should be noted that while most modern apparatus are equipped with brakes on all of the wheels, activation of the parking brake only affects the rear wheels. When the parking brake is applied, the service brakes are released on the front wheels.

On new apparatus, the parking brake must be able to hold a fully loaded apparatus in a steady position on a 20-percent grade. Departments may specify that the parking brake control be located in a position that is accessible to both the driver and the front-seat passenger. This is beneficial in the event the driver becomes incapacitated while driving the vehicle. In this event, the front seat passenger can reach the parking brake control, apply it, and bring the vehicle to a stop.

NFPA 1901 requires apparatus with a GVWR exceeding 36,000 pounds to be equipped with an auxiliary braking system. The standard also recommends them on all vehicles over 32,000 pounds GVWR. These systems may be re quired on lighter apparatus if the department's response districts contain severe grades, congested driving/traffic conditions, or if the apparatus makes a high number of responses. Depending on their design, auxiliary braking systems begin to slow the apparatus as soon as the driver removes his or her foot from the throttle pedal or when pressure is applied to the brake pedal. By beginning the process of slowing the vehicle, the auxiliary brakes reduce the amount of effort required by the service braking system to slow or stop the vehicle. This also helps to reduce the problems associated with brake fade that were dis cussed earlier in this section. If the antilock braking system senses that the vehicle's wheels begin to lock up and a skid is imminent, it will automatically shut down the auxiliary braking system to help avoid this situation. There are a variety of auxiliary braking systems available on fire apparatus, including:

- engine retarders;
- transmission retarders;
- exhaust retarders; and
- driveline retarders.

These systems must be operated as specified by the manufacturer of the system or the apparatus. This includes disabling those systems that are not safe when operated on slippery road surfaces. For more information of types of auxiliary braking systems, see the manufacturer's information or IFSTA's *Pumping Apparatus Driver/Operator Handbook*.

CHASSIS AND VEHICLE WEIGHT CONSIDERATIONS
An important aspect of fire apparatus design is to make sure that the weight bearing capacity of the apparatus chassis is sufficient for the load that is to be placed on it. Apparatus that have loads exceeding the vehicle's GVWR (for straight chassis tankers) or GCWR (gross combination weight rating for trac tor-trailer tankers) are subject to excessive wear, poor steering, brake failures, and a reduced life span. In addition to the GVWR and GCWR, manufacturer's should also ensure that neither front or rear axles are individually overloaded. Front axles must not exceed the front gross axle weight rating (FGAWR), and the rear axle(s) must not exceed the rear gross axle weight rating (RGAWR).

When discussing the vehicle's GVWR or GCWR, it must be understood that we are not simply talking about the vehicle's chassis frame by itself. The vehicle's rated weight capacity is based on a combination of factors, including each of the following:

- chassis frame;

- axles (including the FGAWR and RGAWR);

- atires and wheels;

- spring and suspension system; and

- weight distribution between the front and rear axles.

The manufacturer of the apparatus must carefully match each of these components during construction so that the resultant system has a sufficient weight rating for the finished apparatus. When considering the weight of the finished apparatus, the following elements must be included in the equations:

- The cab and body of the apparatus.

- The amount of water and/or foam concentrate to be carried on the apparatus.

- The amount of portable equipment to be carried on the apparatus (NFPA 1901 requires tankers to allow for at least 1,000 pounds of portable equipment).

- The weight of personnel riding on the apparatus (NFPA 1901 uses 200 pounds per person for each riding position on the apparatus).

NFPA 1901 requires the apparatus to have a weight GVWR or GCWR and a gross axle weight rating (GAWR) label affixed to the apparatus. Before accepting delivery of a new apparatus, the purchaser should verify that the vehicle's weight does not exceed the posted limits.

While most fire service personnel are familiar with the concepts and requirements concerning gross vehicle weights and axle weight requirements, less known but equally important is the vehicle's bridge gross weight. The bridge gross weight rating combines the vehicle's weight with the spacing between its axles. From an apparatus design standpoint, when crossing bridges the axle spacing is equally as important as axle weights. Simply stated, the farther a load is spread out, the less likely it will be to cause damage to a bridge or, for that matter, any road surface. This concept is exemplified in **Figures 4-12 a & b.** In both of these illustrations the truck is carrying the same amount of weight. However, as Figure 4-12a shows, the long truck causes much less stress on the bridge than that caused by the short truck in Figure 4-12b.

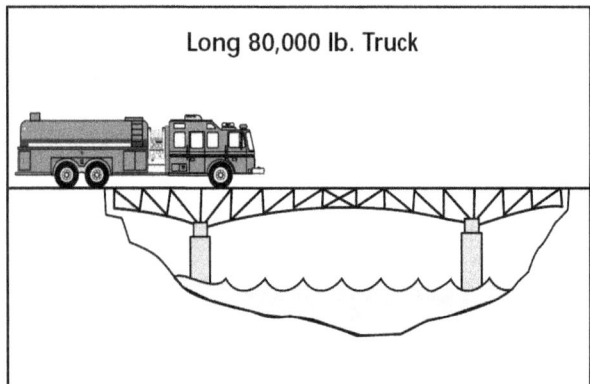

Figure 4-12a By spreading the weight out over a long chassis, there is less stress placed on the bridge.

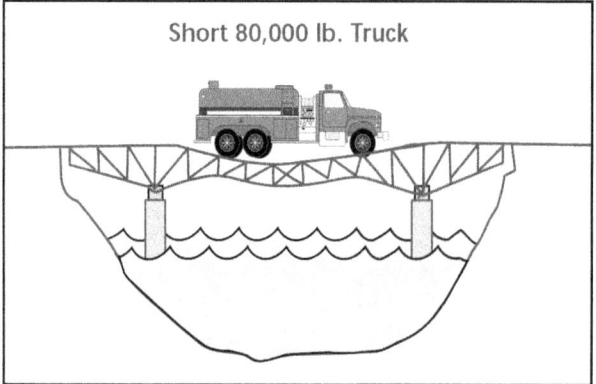

Figure 4-12b An excessive amount of weight on a short chassis may overstress a bridge.

SAFE OPERATION OF FIRE TANKERS

The U.S. Department of Transportation (DOT) uses a bridge gross weight formula to determine the safe bridge weights for trucks. Calculation of this data is too detailed to be covered in this report. However, apparatus purchasers should be familiar with the concept of bridge gross weights and attempt to keep their apparatus within these parameters. For more information on bridge gross weights and their calculation, obtain the document entitled *Bridge Gross Weight Formula* (HTO-33/Rev.4-84) from the DOT (www.dot.gov).

WATER TANK DESIGN AND MOUNTING

Because tanker's primary missions are to haul large quantities of water to emergency scenes, the design and mounting arrangements for their water tanks are of greater interest than they are on other types of fire apparatus. As mentioned earlier in this manual, each gallon of water weighs approximately 8.3 pounds. Thus, each 1,000 gallons of water that the truck carries adds approximately 4½ tons of weight to the apparatus. That means a 3,000-gallon tanker is carrying nearly 13 tons of water.

Keeping in mind that water is very fluid, it becomes obvious that we must design water tanks to control the movement of the water being stored within them. Otherwise inertia and other forces can cause the water to force the vehicle in the same direction that the water is moving. In almost every case, this will work against the driver's ability to control the vehicle. When going around a curve in the road, this motion may cause the tanker to leave the road's surface and/or overturn. When trying to stop the apparatus, it may overpower the vehicle's braking system and cause it to skid or lurch forward.

Water tanks for tankers must be constructed of a noncorrosive material. If the tank is an integral part of the apparatus body, sometimes referred to as a "wet side" tanker, it must also be resistant to condensation. The tank should be mounted securely to the apparatus chassis and is cushioned or cradled in such a manner as to prevent excessive stress on the tank during road travel. The exact shape of the tank will vary depending on the design of the apparatus. Common water tank shapes include

- elliptical;
- t-shaped;
- rectangular; and
- round.

Round and elliptical shaped tanks are most commonly found on standard tankers. Rectangular and T-shaped tanks are more commonly found on pumper-tankers, though exceptions to both rules are somewhat common. In either case, the purchaser and the manufacturer should select a tank that allows for the lowest possible mounting and travel height. This will help keep the apparatus' center of gravity as low as possible and reduce the apparatus' tendency to want to tip over when taking sharp curves in the road.

However, the most crucial aspect of water tank design relative to the safe operation of the apparatus is the use of dividers, called baffles or swash plates, within the tank to control the movement of water during road travel. Properly installed baffles prevent excessive longitudinal and lateral movement of water within the tank. This prevents a liquid surge from occurring and causing the loss of control of the apparatus. There are two primary design methods for installing dividers with any fire apparatus water tank:

- *The Containment Method* -- This method uses a series of swash plates to divide the tank into a series of smaller, interconnected compartments.

- *The Dynamic Method* -- This method uses a series of baffles to disrupt the movement of water by changing its direction of travel. These baffles are often in a staggered so that the changing direction of the water creates a turbulent motion that results in the water absorbing much of its own energy.

In either method of tank design, the dividers that are used within the tank must cover at least 75 percent of the area of the plane that contains the divider. In no case should the distance between dividers or between a divider and a tank wall exceed 48 inches. By following these simple requirements, all of which are contained in NFPA 1901, most accidents caused by liquid surge within the tank can be prevented.

Used/Retrofit Apparatus

As mentioned earlier in this report, rarely are design issues the cause of crashes involving new or manufacturer-built tankers. In contrast, numerous tanker crashes involving used, retrofit, or homebuilt apparatus have had their roots traced back to design concerns or flaws on the apparatus. Most often, these crashes involve tankers from small or rural fire departments that have the need for tankers, but not the funds to purchase new or custom-built apparatus. In an effort to develop a useable tanker within the budget constraints of the their department, the end result is often building a tanker that is not particularly roadworthy or safe. Three scenarios that often lead to problems are

- Converting an existing fire apparatus, such as a pumper or rescue vehicle, into a tanker **(Figure 4-13)**. This often occurs when a department acquires a new pumper or rescue vehicle and decides that the vehicle being replaced could be made more useful by converting it into a tanker. Removing or modifying the vehicle's original fire body so that it will accept a larger water tank accomplishes this.

- Converting a fuel, milk, or other type of tanker into a fire department tanker **(Figure 4-14)**. This is often accomplished with little significant modifications to the vehicle.

- Converting a military surplus vehicle, such as 6x6, 2½ ton, or aircraft refueling trucks into a tanker **(Figure 4-15)**. This is often accomplished by adding a homebuilt or other non-fire service designed tank to the bed of the apparatus.

Converting any vehicle, whether it be a piece of fire apparatus, a non-fire service tanker, or a military surplus vehicle is not the preferred manner for obtaining a reliable fire department tanker. As much as possible this practice should be avoided. The reason that most of these vehicles are being made available to the fire department is because they have outlived their useful service life with the original owner. In other words, the vehicle is probably

Figure 4-13 In this case, the FDNY converted pumpers that originally carried 500 gallons of water to foam tankers that carry 1,000 gallons of foam concentrate. This conversion did include chassis and brake system upgrades.
Courtesy of Ron Jeffers

Figure 4-14 A civilian fuel tanker converted for fire department use.

Figure 4-15 A surplus military 6x6 vehicle converted into a fire department tanker.

already worn out. To then take this worn-out vehicle and place the enormous amount of weight on it that a fire department tanker carries further com pounds the questionable roadworthiness of the vehicle. If the fire department does not have the means to purchase a properly engineered tanker, any homebuilt or retrofit tanker they construct should be designed so that it meets the intent of the NFPA 1901 standard.

In reviewing the crash statistics and case studies covered earlier in this manual, a number of particular areas of concern regarding retrofit and homebuilt tankers emerge. The following sections highlight some of these con cerns and provide information on how they can be avoided.

CHASSIS AND VEHICLE WEIGHT CONSIDERATIONS

Perhaps the most common safety issue affecting tankers made from used or retrofit vehicles involves the tendency for them to be seriously overweight when filled with water. Many agencies fail to design and build the vehicle so that it stays within its designed GVWR. In some cases, the vehicle grossly exceeds the GVWR. The result is a vehicle that will be subject to frequent mechanical break-downs, will be difficult to steer, and will have insufficient braking abilities when fully loaded with water. Unless the vehicle's suspension system, chassis, axles, tires, and braking system are upgraded during the conversion process, the vehicle must be designed so that its original GVWR is not exceeded. This type of upgrading is a very complex and expensive process; in most cases, it is more effective to simply buy a new chassis.

Converting an existing fire apparatus, such as a pumper or aerial appara tus, into a tanker can result in immediate problems. In its previous life, the vehicle was engineered specifically to carry the weight of the pumper body, equipment, and water, or the rescue body and equipment. In both cases, this is typically substantially less weight than that associated with a tanker. If the existing fire body is removed and a large capacity tank is mounted onto the chassis, in almost every case the vehicle will greatly exceed its GVWR. If you wish to convert an existing apparatus to a tanker, consult the original manu facturer of the fire apparatus to determine how this can be done safely. The manufacturer may be able to provide you with information on the maximum tank capacity and body size that may be suitable for the existing chassis or how the chassis can be upgraded to accept a larger water tank and body.

Small fire departments often acquire used tankers from fuel companies or the military. In theory, this allows them to make a fairly quick and simple conversion to a fire apparatus. However, even though these vehicles come ready equipped with a large capacity tank, they may not have the GVWR sufficient to allow them to operate safely as a fire department tanker. Water weighs approximately 8.3 pounds per gallon. Most fuel products hauled by tankers have a weight ranging from 6.75 to 7.5 pounds per gallon. For purposes of example, suppose a 3,000-gallon tanker was designed primarily to haul a grade of fuel that weighs 7.3 pounds per gallon. Thus, when filled with water this vehicle weighs 3,000 pounds more than when it was filled with fuel. Again, before converting these vehicles for fire department use, determine the vehicle's GVWR and do not exceed it.

Very serious overweight situations and accidents have occurred involving tankers that were constructed from surplus military 2½-ton (often called *deuce and a half*) vehicles. First of all, keep in mind that the reason these vehicles are offered at surplus auctions is because they are usually worn out and no longer suitable for military use. Secondly, these vehicles were originally designed to be personnel carriers, not heavy-load- hauling vehicles. To greatly overload any vehicle is dangerous; however, to overload one that was not particularly roadworthy or designed to carry heavy loads to begin with is a recipe for disas ter.

The reason these types of vehicles are called 2½-ton or deuce and a half vehicles is because that is their rated maximum load capacity. That means that the combined weight of the water, tank, equipment, and people riding on the apparatus must not exceed 5,000 pounds. Because water weighs 8.3 pounds per gallon, 5,000 pounds of water equals about 600 gallons. However, the amount of water that may be safely carried will be substantially less than that when factoring in the other elements. Some fire departments have placed these deuce and a half vehicles into service with water tanks that carry 1,000- to 2,000-gallon water tanks on them. This is extremely dangerous as it could result in a vehicle that is 300 to 400 percent over legal or safe weight. Vehicles that are this much overweight should be removed from service immediately.

BRAKING SYSTEM CONSIDERATIONS

When converting or retrofitting a vehicle to become a fire department tanker, the capabilities and condition of the vehicle's braking system is as important as the chassis and weight limit considerations. As discussed in the section on new fire apparatus, the braking system is perhaps one of the most important mechanical systems related to operating the vehicle safely. This system must be thoroughly analyzed before placing a retrofit or converted vehicle into ser vice as a tanker.

In much the same manner as described above for chassis and weight carry ing capacity, the braking system on a vehicle that is intended to be converted into a tanker was probably designed for the vehicle's original use. The system, as it was originally designed, may not have sufficient braking capabilities to safely serve as a fire department tanker. Typically, fire department vehicles brake more frequently and more harshly than standard commercial vehicles.

Standard braking systems may overheat or have insufficient air pressure ca
pacities to allow safe operation during the conditions associated with an
emergency response. Either of these conditions may cause the brakes to become "mushy" or fade and lose their capability to safely slow or stop the vehicle.
Even vehicles that previously served as fuel or milk tankers may not have a
braking system suitable for an emergency vehicle.

The manufacturer of the vehicle's chassis and/or braking system should be
consulted when retrofitting a vehicle to become a fire department tanker. These
sources should be able to provide reliable information on what adjustments or
system upgrades will be needed in order to ensure that the vehicle will be safe
once it is placed in service as a fire department tanker.

WATER TANK DESIGN AND MOUNTING CONSIDERATIONS

Because it will carry the most significant part of the vehicle's load once the
tanker is placed in service, significant consideration must be given to the design of the water tank and how it will be mounted on the vehicle. Numerous
fire department tanker accidents can have their causes traced back to prob
lems associated with the vehicle's water tank.

Fire departments must ensure that any tank that is constructed to be placed
on a retrofit vehicle is designed in accordance with the water tank require
ments contained in NFPA 1901. The most common deficiency associated with
tanks that have been constructed for use on retrofit tankers is improper and
insufficient tank baffling. The hazards associated with improper baffling were
discussed in the section on water tanks for new apparatus. Most reputable
companies that build water tanks for fire apparatus on a regular basis will be
familiar with the baffling requirements contained in NFPA 1901, and they will
follow them in every case. However, this may not be the case with a local
welding firm or other type of business that may offer to assist a fire depart
ment operating on a limited budget by building a tank for them. If the party
seeking to build the tank is unable to construct it to the requirements of NFPA
1901, their offer should not be accepted.

It must also be noted that it is quite common for fuel or milk tankers that
are being converted for fire department use to have insufficient tank baffling
to allow them to safely operate as an emergency vehicle. Some fuel tankers
may have limited baffling, but not enough to control water during the rigor
ous conditions of an emergency response. This is often the case with tankers
that are intended to carry two or more different types or grades of fuel. In some
cases, the only baffles that these tanks have are the divider walls between the
different storage compartments. Fuel tanks must be inspected prior to use as a
fire department tanker to ensure that the baffling is adequate. If it is found not
to be adequate, corrections must be made before placing it in service for fire
department use.

It is quite common for milk tankers to have no baffles inside their tanks
whatsoever. The lack of baffles is related to sanitary concerns for hauling milk.
The presence of baffles makes complete sterilization of the tank increasingly
difficult. Obviously, sterilization is a huge concern for dairy companies, so the
baffles are omitted from their tanks. Drivers of milk tankers are aware of the

lack of baffles and operate the vehicle accordingly. Again, before these vehicles can safely be converted for fire department use, a thorough analysis of the tank's interior must be conducted, and it must be brought into compliance with the baffling requirements contained in NFPA 1901.

The next design consideration that must be analyzed before placing a converted vehicle into service as a fire department tanker is the location the tank is to be mounted on the vehicle. This is particularly true if the vehicle was not equipped with a tank during its previous use. The following is a synopsis of the mounting location arrangements that must be considered

- The tank should be mounted so that the weight of the tank and water is distributed over the entire length of the vehicle as much as possible. If the tank is mounted in such a manner as to place an inordinate amount of weight on the rear axle(s), it could result in a vehicle that is difficult to steer or otherwise control **(Figure 4-16)**.

- The tank should be mounted in a manner that results in the vehicle's center of gravity being maintained as low as possible. Creating vehicles with a dangerously high center of gravity is particularly a problem when retrofitting surplus military vehicles into use as fire department tankers. Often, the fire department places the tank on top of the flat bed body that the vehicle came equipped with. Some tanks have a cradle or legs that keep the bottom of the tank several inches to more than a foot above the bed of the vehicle. This results in a vehicle with an exceptionally high center of gravity and one that may not handle safely when making quick movements during an emergency response **(Figure 4-17)**. All efforts must be made to make the vehicle's center of gravity as low as possible.

Again, even vehicles that previously served as fuel or milk tankers may have center or gravity problems when operated as a fire department tanker. Those vehicles were not designed for the type of driving conditions encountered by emergency vehicles. They may have a high center of gravity that causes the tanker to overturn when operated in an emergency response condition.

Figure 4-16 Although not always the case, one sign of an overloaded chassis is excessive sagging of the body over the rear wheels.

Figure 4-17 Note that the cradle legs between these tanks and the truck bed actually raise the vehicle's center of gravity even further.

The last factor that needs to be evaluated relative to water tanks on retrofit fire department tankers is the manner in which they are attached to the vehicle. Fire department must ensure that the tank is completely secured to the vehicle. Cases have been noted where tanks were not properly secured to the vehicle and came loose during road travel.

Apparatus Visibility Issues

For most of the North American fire service's first 200 or so years, the issue of apparatus color and visibility could more accurately have been described as a nonissue. However, beginning in the late 1960's and early 1970's, a number of factors led the fire service to explore the issue of visibility. These factors included rising incidences of fire apparatus crashes and research that was being conducted on how vehicle visibility affects its chances of being involved in a crash. The primary issues associated with fire apparatus visibility include apparatus color, warning lights, and reflective marking. The following sections highlight the important facts involving each of these.

APPARATUS COLOR

In the first 200 years or so of the North American fire service, the vast majority of fire apparatus was painted red as part of a tradition whose roots traced to the first days of the fire service. There is disagreement on how the color red became associated with fire apparatus. Some theories state that people associate the color red with fire. Others involve the fact that most early vehicles were black in color and red would stand out. This was particularly important in the days before warning lights were widely available and used.

By 1970, it was estimated that 85 percent of all fire apparatus in the United States was painted red. Communities that did deviate from the industry-wide tradition of red apparatus generally did so in favor of recognizing a local tradition. Many of these local traditions have remained intact for 100 years or more.

In the mid-1970's, research conducted by a New York eye doctor indicated that the best color choice for fire apparatus and emergency vehicles was yellow or lime-yellow. This was based on the fact that the human eye is most sensitive to a narrow band of colors between the wavelengths of 510 mμ (millimicrons) and 570 mμ . Yellow and lime-yellow fall into this range. These colors are highly visible and distinguishable from background clutter during both day and night conditions. Few other vehicles on the road were painted these colors (because most people thought lime-yellow, in particular, was ugly), so most people would learn to identify them with an emergency vehicle. Numerous departments were influenced by this research, and it is estimated that somewhere between 20 and 50 percent of American fire apparatus constructed in the 1970's and early 1980's bore the lime-yellow color scheme.

Over time, fire departments that experimented with the conversion to the lime-yellow color determined that it had little measurable effect on improving their response times or reducing their accident rates. By the mid 1980's many of the departments that had experimented with or completely switched over to lime-yellow apparatus were making the conversion back to their traditional colors (usually red).

In summary, scientific evidence proves that red is not the most visible color to the human eye. Technically, lime-yellow fire apparatus are more visible than other colors. However, there is no conclusive evidence showing that the color of fire apparatus has a dramatic effect on the likelihood of the apparatus being involved in a crash. Therefore, most fire departments have chosen to base the color of their apparatus on the traditions that exist in their communities. Most experts agree on one fact: how the apparatus is driven has a much larger impact on the likelihood of the apparatus being involved in a crash than does the color. If the driver places the vehicle in a position where the color of the vehicle will be the deciding factor on whether or not it will be involved in a crash, one or more serious, usually preventable errors has already occurred.

WARNING LIGHTS

NFPA 1901 contains detailed requirements for warning lights that are to be placed on fire apparatus. Because of the detailed nature of these requirements, it is not possible to summarize them in the space allotted in this publication. However, we can look at some of the basic issues surrounding apparatus and firefighter safety with respect to warning lights and basic steps that can be used to improve that safety.

Early fire apparatus were typically not equipped with a significant amount of warning lights. In reality, the need for warning lights was not particularly crucial because the amount of traffic on the road in those days was relatively light and background clutter and lights were not nearly as substantial as is in today's society. By the 1980's and the 1990's, fire apparatus were typically equipped with a dazzling array of rotating lights, flashers, alternating headlights, and strobe lights covering every portion of the apparatus, top to bottom, corner to corner (**Figure 4-18**).

Figure 4-18 Apparatus with large numbers of warning lights may pose hazards when parked on the emergency scene. *Courtesy of Joel Woods, Maryland Fire & Rescue Institute*

The addition of all of these warning lights resulted in little or no improvement in fire apparatus crash rates. Fire departments began to recognize that the abundant use of warning lights could have actually contributed to some crashes. Numerous minor and major apparatus crash investigations cited blinding of the oncoming civilian driver by flashing headlights or excessive warning lights as a reason for the crashes.

During this period, the Phoenix, Arizona, Fire Department conducted a study involving the use of warning lights when parked on the emergency scene. This study was initiated following the death of a firefighter while loading a patient into the back of an ambulance on a "routine" medical response. A drunk driver struck the firefighter. The Phoenix study developed several important conclusions:

- The use of the full array of warning lights during the emergency response does improve the visibility of the vehicle, as long as none of those lights blind other drivers.

- The use of the full array of warning lights while parked on the emergency scene may create a hazardous condition for personnel operating on the scene. A large amount of warning lights overpowers the oncoming driver's ability to see personnel standing around the vehicles. Furthermore, the excessive amount of light flashing toward the oncoming driver negates the effectiveness of retroreflective markings on the firefighters turnout cloth ing or safety vests.

- When parked on the emergency scene, it is advisable to turn off most of the warning lights used on the emergency response. One or two small rotating amber lights should be left on to draw the attention of oncoming drivers, without blinding them or neutralizing firefighter reflective markings.

- Headlights facing oncoming traffic should be turned off.

The following is a summary of good practices related to emergency vehicle warning lights, apparatus, and firefighter safety. These measures should be implemented as much as possible by each jurisdiction.

- If possible, all new, existing, and retrofit fire apparatus should have emer gency warning lights conforming to the standards contained in NFPA 1901.

- Jurisdictions should ensure that the warning lights on its apparatus con form to their State's motor vehicle code. Each State has different requirements for warning lights on emergency vehicles. These require ments may include things such as limiting the colors of warning lights that may be used on particular vehicles, limiting the use of white flashing lights or flashing headlights, or other similar issues.

- Apparatus should be equipped with a combination of rotating incandes cent and flashing strobe lights. The rotating lights are more visible than strobes during daylight hours and the opposite is true at night.

- Apparatus should be equipped with one or two small rotating amber lights that can be left on when the apparatus is parked on the emergency scene during night operations. All other warning lights should be turned off.

- Headlights should be turned off when parked on the emergency scene if there is a possibility that they could blind oncoming drivers.

- Alternating or otherwise flashing headlights should be used for daytime responses only. They are very effective in gaining the attention of oncom ing drivers in daylight. However, they may blind oncoming drivers at night and may also make operating the apparatus more difficult.

- When responding in snow or fog, forward-facing strobe or oscillating lights should be turned off to reduce visual disorientation of the apparatus driver.

Again, consult NFPA 1901 for more detailed information on apparatus warn ing lights.

REFLECTIVE MARKINGS

Reflective markings, sometimes referred to as retroreflective markings, are a third means used to increase the visibility of the fire apparatus (**Figure 4-19**). NFPA 1901 contains the following requirements for reflective markings to be placed on all new fire apparatus:

Figure 4-19 All new fire apparatus are required to have reflective trim down the side of the apparatus.

Figure 4-20 Reflective graphic designs may take the place of simple reflective trim. *Courtesy of Ron Bogardus*

- A reflective stripe, or combination of stripes, totaling minimum width of 4 inches conforming to the standards set forth in ASTM D 4956, *Standard Specifications for Retroreflective Sheeting for Traffic Control*, Type I, Class 1 or 3, must be used. More information on this standard is available at www.astm.org.

- The stripe should run at least 50 percent of the cab and body length on each side of the apparatus.

- The stripe should run at least 50 percent of the body width on the rear of the apparatus.

- The stripe should run at least 25 percent of the body width on the front of the apparatus.

- A graphic design may be used in place of a plain stripe as long as the coverage of the design is equal to or exceeds the minimum area required covered by the standard (**Figure 4-20**).

It must be kept in mind that reflective striping is only effective during nighttime operations and only when the headlight beams of the oncoming vehicle come into range of the reflective material. The effectiveness of the reflective marking is reduced if the civilian vehicle is approaching the apparatus from an angle as opposed to straight on. The general practice is to locate these stripes on the fire apparatus at about same height as the typical headlights for oncoming vehicles.

In recent years some fire departments have started using extensive reflective markings on the rear of the apparatus to increase visibility and safety (**Figure 4-21**). These markings generally cover the entire rear of the apparatus with a combination of luminescent orange paint and retroreflective black cross-hash markings. This style of marking is common on European fire apparatus and U.S. highway department and public utility vehicles. The practice was too new at the time of this article to note if any significant effect on crash rates will be realized by these changes.

Figure 4-21 Some newer apparatus are being outfitted with European-type reflective markings on the back of the apparatus. *Courtesy of Bob Barraclough*

SAFE OPERATION OF FIRE TANKERS

SAFE APPARATUS DRIVING PRACTICES

Certainly, the apparatus design and maintenance issues discussed to this point in the chapter are important from the overall standpoint of fire apparatus crash avoidance and firefighter safety. However, the single most important issue that affects crash avoidance and safety is the manner in which the vehicle is driven to and from the emergency scene. As stated above, only 5 percent of all apparatus crashes are caused by mechanical failures. A few more are caused when a parked fire apparatus is struck by another vehicle. The *vast* majority of apparatus crashes occur while the apparatus is moving. In this section of the chapter, we will examine safe driving practices that can be used to significantly lower the chance of an apparatus being involved in a crash.

Driving at an Appropriate Speed

A significant percentage of crashes involving fire department tankers is attributed to the vehicle being driven at an excessive speed for the given conditions. Driving the tanker at an excessive speed may result in any one of the following scenarios occurring:

- The tanker is unable to stop before hitting another vehicle or fixed object.
- The tanker leaves the roadway when negotiating a curve.
- Centrifugal force or a load shift causes the tanker to overturn when negotiating a curve.

The potential for any of these scenarios to occur may be increased by road surfaces that are wet, icy, unpaved, contain loose impediments, or are banked in one direction or the other. Drivers must recognize these dangerous conditions and adjust for them accordingly. The vehicle must always be driven at a speed that allows it to be maintained under control, on the roadway, and able to stop within a reasonable distance. This speed will need to be reduced if the road is wet, icy, or unpaved.

During training, the driver should develop a sense of what the safest maximum speed for operating the tanker is under a variety of conditions. Training should begin at low speeds and increase only as the driver becomes more comfortable driving the apparatus. Difficult routes of travel within the response district should be included in road testing so that the driver will understand how the vehicle will handle when making an emergency response.

Many fire departments have established policies on the maximum speed at which the apparatus may be driven during an emergency response. Drivers should be reminded that the *established* maximum speed is not the *required* maximum speed. In other words, the driver should not drive at the maximum speed if he or she does not feel that he or she can safely control the vehicle at that speed. While many State motor vehicle codes or fire department operating procedures allow emergency vehicles to exceed the posted or cautionary speed limit during an emergency response, this practice is not recommended for fire department tankers.

In many cases the fire department tanker is the 3rd or 4th due piece of apparatus on the scene. It is a support vehicle, not an attack vehicle (unless it is a pumper-tanker being operated as an attack pumper). It is better to arrive a few seconds later than not at all. If first-arriving units determine that no serious condition exists, the Incident Commander (IC) should order all en route apparatus, including tankers, to proceed at a nonemergency rate of speed. It is irresponsible to have vehicles continue an emergency response when no emergency exists.

The driver also should never heed any request by the fire officer on board the apparatus to increase its speed beyond the point that the driver is comfortable controlling it. On the contrary, the officer, or any other passenger riding next to the driver, also should be observant to the speed the vehicle is being driven and recommend that the driver slow down if it is felt that the apparatus may be in danger. Some fire departments place a second speedometer on the officer's side of the vehicle so that the passenger can more accurately keep an eye on the actual speed the vehicle is being driven (**Figure 4-22**).

Figure 4-22 By placing a speedometer on the right side of the dashboard, the apparatus officer can more easily monitor the apparatus speed.

Safe Stopping Distances

Closely tied to the concept of driving the apparatus at an appropriate speed is the driver's understanding of the braking and stopping capabilities of the tanker. A driver should have a working knowledge of the total stopping distance of the tanker. The *total stopping distance* is the sum of the driver perception distance, the driver reaction distance, the brake lag distance, and the vehicle braking distance (**Figure 4-23**). These distances can be summarized as follows:

- The driver *perception distance* is the distance a vehicle travels between when the need to brake occurs and when the driver recognizes this need.

- The driver *reaction distance* is the distance a vehicle travels while a driver is transferring the foot from the accelerator to the brake pedal after perceiving the need for stopping.

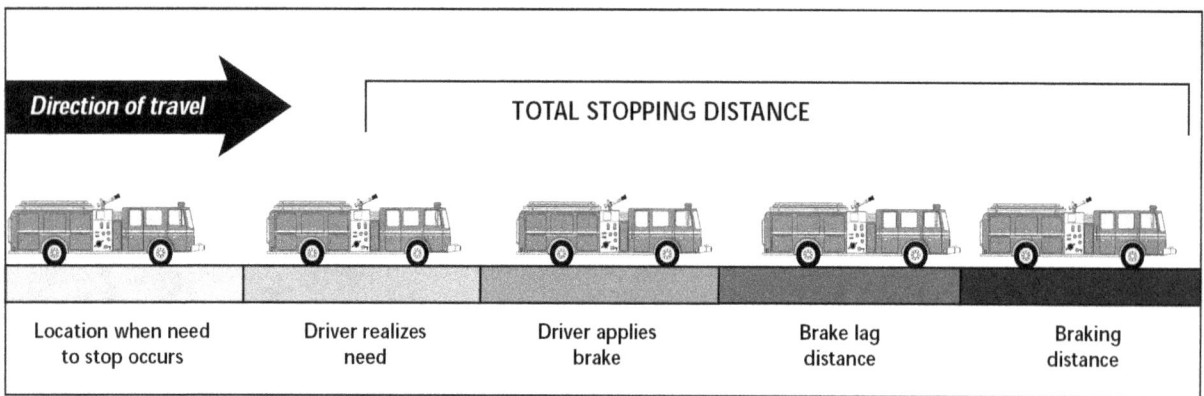

Figure 4-23 A diagram of the total stopping distance for a vehicle. Note that in reality these portions are not equidistant.

- The *brake lag distance* is the distance the apparatus travels from the time the driver applies pressure to the brake pedal and the brake system begins to slow the apparatus.
- The *braking distance* is the distance the vehicle travels from the time the brakes begin to slow the apparatus until the apparatus comes to a complete stop.

Each department should conduct braking distance tests with its own apparatus. As well, drivers should test the apparatus on their own so that they have a firsthand understanding of the apparatus' capabilities.

There are a number of factors that influence the driver's ability to stop the tanker:
- condition of the driving surface;
- speed being traveled;
- weight of the vehicle;
- type and condition of the vehicle's braking system and tires;
- whether the vehicle is being driven uphill or downhill;
- water surge that occurs within the water tank; and
- whether the vehicle has a manual or automatic transmission.

A dry, paved road provides the optimal stopping ability from a driving surface standpoint. The ability of the apparatus to stop is negatively affected by wet, snowy, icy, or unpaved roads. As mentioned above, drivers must compensate for these conditions by reducing their speeds by an appropriate amount to match the conditions.

The correlation between vehicle weight and speed and stopping distance is simple. At an equal speed, it will take a greater distance to stop a large tanker than it will a brush pumper. It will also take a greater distance to stop a vehicle that is going 50 mph (80 km/h) than the same vehicle when it is traveling 30 mph (48 km/h). These two factors exemplify the need for the driver to train on the exact vehicle he or she will be expected to drive under emergency response conditions. A driver who certified on a pumper may not have a working understanding of the handling characteristics of a large tanker.

The type and condition of the braking system has a tremendous impact on the ability to stop the fire apparatus. For example, in the case of air brakes, there is a slight delay in the time from which the driver pushes down on the brake pedal until sufficient air pressure is sent to the brake to operate. This must be considered when determining total stopping distance.

Several serious fire apparatus accidents have been traced to poor maintenance of the braking system and/or tires. Obviously, a vehicle that has a properly maintained braking system will stop faster than one that has a system in disrepair. Tires that are in good condition will also provide better traction and reduce the stopping distance. Braking systems and maintenance programs were discussed earlier in this chapter.

The forces of gravity will affect the tanker's ability to stop depending on whether the tanker is going up or down a hill. Gravity will assist the tanker in stopping quicker when traveling uphill. Conversely, the tanker's stopping distance will be increased when traveling downhill.

Water surge within the apparatus water tank will also work against the stopping ability of the tanker. When the apparatus brakes are applied, water in the tank will surge toward the front of the truck. This effect will be greater in improperly baffled tanks, but it occurs in all tanks to some extent. Keep in mind that a 3,000-gallon tanker is carrying roughly 25,000 pounds of water. The force of this moving weight will cause inertia that increases the stopping distance of the vehicle. In severe cases, it has been known to cause the vehicle to skid or lunge forward even after the vehicle's wheels have stopped turning.

Unimproved Road Surfaces

Many fire departments, particularly those in rural areas, have unpaved or otherwise unimproved roads within their jurisdictions. Through preincident planning and response district surveys, the fire department should determine which roads will safely handle the weight of the fire department tanker and which roads are unsuitable to be used for an emergency response. The district should be surveyed during dry and rainy conditions, as some roads that may be suitable during dry weather may become impassable during wet weather.

It is also very common for unpaved roads to contain low weight restriction bridges at locations where the road crosses bodies of water or trenches. Many of these bridges will not support the weight of a fire department tanker (or any other large fire apparatus for that matter). These bridges must be identified in preincident planning and alternative routes around them must be made known to the drivers. It may actually be quicker to have mutual or automatic aid tankers located on the opposite side of the bridge to respond than it would be for the closer tanker to take an alternative route around the bridge. Alternative water supply sources on the far side of these bridges should also be noted in preincident plans.

Even if an unpaved road is deemed safe for operation of the tanker, the driver generally must drive the vehicle at a considerably slower speed than the tanker would be driven on a paved road. Some of the reasons this is necessary are:

- The unpaved road surface will consist of dirt, loose gravel, or similar material. These surfaces may enhance the vehicle's tendency to skid or slide in marginal control situations.

- These roads often have ruts in the locations that vehicle wheels most commonly travel. These ruts can adversely affect the control of the tanker if the vehicle moves in and out of them **(Figure 4-24)**.

Figure 4-24 Ruts can easily develop over time in unpaved roads.

SAFE OPERATION OF FIRE TANKERS

- Poorly maintained unpaved roads may have serious potholes, gulleys, or other deformities **(Figure 4.25)**. Striking these deformities at an unsafe speed may cause the driver to lose control of the vehicle. Some roads develop a sort of "washboard" pattern in their surface that will cause the apparatus to go into a rhythmic bouncing if driven too fast across them. This bouncing adversely affects the driver's ability to slow or steer the vehicle.

Because of their large size and heavy weight, it is generally not recommended that fire department tankers be driven off the road. If they are being used to resupply wildland fire apparatus that are engaged in off-road firefighting, the wildland apparatus should drive out to the road to meet the tanker when they need to be refilled.

Figure 4-25 Be alert for serious deformities in unpaved roads.

Avoiding Skids

The most effective way to combat apparatus skids is to avoid them altogether. The most common causes of skids involve driver error, including:

- Driving too fast for road conditions.
- Failing to properly appreciate weight shifts of heavy apparatus.
- Failing to anticipate obstacles (these range from other vehicles to animals).
- Improper use of auxiliary braking devices.
- Improper maintenance of tire air pressure and adequate tread depth. Tires that are overinflated or lacking in reasonable tread depth make the apparatus more susceptible to skids. The proper tire pressure should be obtained from the *Tire and Rim Year Book* published by the Tire and Rim Association, Inc. Do not obtain tire pressure from the sidewall of the tire.

Most newer, large fire apparatus are equipped with an all-wheel, antilock braking system (ABS) that is powered by air pressure. These systems minimize the chance of the vehicle being put into a skid when the brakes are applied forcefully. An onboard computer that monitors each wheel controls air pressure to the brakes, maintaining optimal braking ability. A sensing device monitors the speed of each wheel. When a wheel begins to lock up, the sensing device sends a signal to the computer that the wheel is not turning. The computer analyzes this signal against the signals from the other wheels to determine if this particular wheel should still be turning. If it is determined that it should be turning, a signal is sent to the air modulation valve at that wheel, reducing the air brake pressure and allowing the wheel to turn. Once the wheel turns, it is braked again. The computer makes these decisions many times a second, until the vehicle is brought to a halt. Because of this mechanical capability, when driving a vehicle equipped with an ABS, maintain a steady pressure on the brake pedal (rather than pumping the pedal) until the apparatus is brought to a complete halt.

Figure 4-26 Skid pads can be used to train drivers in controlling the vehicle under adverse weather conditions.

On vehicles that are equipped with both an antilock braking system and an auxiliary braking system, the computer controlling the *antilock* braking system will shut off the *auxiliary* braking system during a skid condition. This will help to reduce the vehicle's tendency to continue the skid.

If an apparatus that is **not** equipped with an ABS goes into a skid, the driver should release the brakes and allow the wheels to rotate freely. Turn the apparatus steering wheel so that the front wheels face in the direction of the skid. If using a standard transmission, do not push in the clutch pedal until the vehicle is under control and just before stopping the vehicle. Once the skid is controllable, gradually apply power to the wheels to further control the vehicle by giving traction.

Skid control skills may be learned through practice on skid pads. These are specially designed, smooth surface driving areas that have water directed onto them to make skids likely **(Figure 4-26)**. All training should be done at slow speeds to avoid damaging the vehicle or injuring participants. Some jurisdictions choose to use reserve apparatus or other older vehicles for this part of the training process.

Negotiating Curves

As we saw in Chapters 2 and 3, tankers have a high incidence rate of being involved in crashes when they are unable to negotiate a curve in the roadway. Almost all of these crashes occur because the tanker enters the curve at an unsafe speed and the driver loses control of the vehicle. This loss of control may result in a number of scenarios:

- The tanker enters oncoming lanes of traffic and strikes another vehicle.
- The tanker partially or completely leaves the roadway.
- A weight shift occurs in the water tank causing the driver to lose control.
- Centrifugal force and/or inertia causes the tanker to overturn.

Specific strategies for dealing with each of the listed scenarios are covered elsewhere in this report. However, once again the best strategy for safely negotiating curves is to maintain control of the vehicle by entering the curve at a reasonable, safe speed. Drivers should be familiar with tricky curves in their response district or potential mutual aid areas and know what the safe speeds are for negotiating them. When driving on unfamiliar roads, be alert for yellow road signs indicating upcoming curves and pay attention to the suggested speeds that are usually found on the bottom portions of these signs. Keep in mind that these suggested speeds are intended for passenger cars traveling on a dry road. Most likely these suggested speeds will be too high for a fire department tanker to safely negotiate the curve. Speeds will need to be further reduced if the road surface is wet or icy.

Traversing Grades

The large size and heavy weight of tankers make driving them up and down hills a little more challenging than with smaller vehicles. The safe practices for operating tankers on hills differ depending on whether the vehicle has a manual or automatic transmission and whether it has an auxiliary braking system.

TANKERS EQUIPPED WITH MANUAL TRANSMISSIONS

Most people do consider driving uphill to be a risky proposition. However, when driving a tanker equipped with a manual transmission uphill, if proper gear shifting principles are not followed, it is possible that the driver will be unable to get the vehicle into any gear. The result could be the vehicle starting to drift backwards down the hill. To prevent this, shift the transmission to a lower gear. This practice provides adequate driving power and enables the driver to keep the apparatus under control.

When driving downhill, select a lower gear and remain in gear at all times. A commonly followed rule of thumb is to use one gear less going downhill than you would use to go up the same hill. The engine provides braking power when the vehicle is in gear. To prevent engine damage, limit downhill speed to lower than maximum governed rpm. The engine governor cannot control engine speed downhill, as the wheels turn the driveshaft and engine. Engine rotation faster than the rated rpm can result in damage to the vehicle's engine and loss of control of the vehicle. For this reason, it is best not to allow the vehicle to coast while going down the hill.

TANKERS EQUIPPED WITH AUTOMATIC TRANSMISSIONS

Traversing up or down grades with a tanker equipped with an automatic transmission is considerably easier than with an apparatus equipped with a manual transmission. Whether going uphill or downhill the transmission system will generally will select the appropriate gear for the apparatus automatically. However, the driver should not overrely on the apparatus to maintain control of the vehicle and should still exercise caution, particularly when going downhill. The driver should use the vehicle's service and auxiliary braking systems to ensure the vehicle maintains a safe speed for the given road conditions.

Adverse Weather Conditions

Though statistics show that the majority of tanker crashes occur on dry roads, weather can play a factor in safe driving. Rain, snow, ice, and mud make roads slippery and more dangerous to negotiate. A driver must recognize these dangers and adjust apparatus speed according to the crown of the road, the sharpness of curves, and the condition of road surfaces. The speed should be decreased gradually when necessary. The driver also should slow down while approaching curves, keep off low or soft shoulders, and avoid sudden turns. Areas that first become slippery include bridge surfaces, northern slopes of hills, shaded spots, and areas where snow is blowing across the roadway.

It is a good policy to try the brakes while in an area free of traffic to find out how slippery the road might be. This will allow the driver to adjust accord ingly when operating in traffic. Speed must be adjusted to road and weather conditions so that the apparatus can be stopped or maneuvered safely. During slippery-road conditions, the safe following distance between vehicles increases dramatically. Remember that it takes 3 to 15 times more distance for a vehicle to come to a complete stop on snow and ice than it does on dry concrete.

Snow tires or tire chains will reduce the stopping distance and considerably increase starting and hill-climbing traction on snow or ice. Apparatus may be

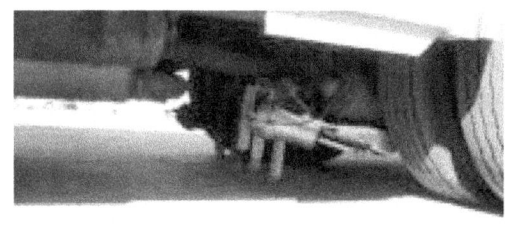
Figure 4-27 Automatic tire chains work fairly well in snow up to about 6 or 8 inches deep.

equipped with the traditional, manually applied tire chains or the newer automatic variety. Automatic tire chains consist of short lengths of chain on a rotating hub in front of each rear wheel **(Figure 4-27)**. The hubs swing down into place when a switch on the dashboard is activated. The rotation of the hub throws the chains underneath the rolling tires. These chains tend to lose their effectiveness in snow that is deeper than 8 inches.

It is also recommended that fire departments allow, if not require, tanker drivers to perform driver training during periods of inclement weather and adverse road conditions. It is not reasonable to expect the drivers to do all of their training on dry roads and then control the vehicle during an emergency response in a snow or rainstorm. Controlled driver training during these conditions is invaluable in providing experience and confidence for the driver during adverse weather.

Regaining Control When Right-Side Wheels Leave the Roadway

A significant number of tanker and other fire department apparatus crashes have occurred as a result of the apparatus drifting off the right side of the road surface. This has occurred both on straight sections of road as well as curves. This situation develops when, for whatever reason, the apparatus drifts too far to the right and the front, rear, or both sets of tires leave the paved surface.

Generally, the simple act of the tires leaving the paved surface does not create a significant hazard in and of itself. It is possible that, if the shoulder is very soft, it could throw the vehicle toward the right into an object along the roadway or perhaps into a rollover situation. However, most crashes that occur when the right side wheels leave the paved surface are as a result of an "overcorrection" and the resultant panic by the driver when attempting to bring the right side wheel(s) back onto the paved surface. Often, there will be a lip of 4 to 8 inches where the paving drops off onto the soft shoulder. When the driver attempts to bring the right-side tires over this lip back onto the paved surface at too high of a speed, the common reaction is for the vehicle to shoot quickly (in some cases violently) toward the left. This could cause the apparatus to enter opposing lanes of traffic, go completely off the left side of the road, or to begin a rocking motion that results in loss of control of the vehicle. In other cases, the vehicle may stay on the roadway, but the jerking action of jumping back onto the paved surface causes the rear end of the vehicle to swing out in a counterclockwise motion, causing the vehicle to overturn.

Drivers must be trained regarding the hazards of drifting off the right side of the paved surface. When either or both of the right-side wheels/tires drift off of the paved surface, the driver should be instructed to slow the vehicle gradually to a safe speed before attempting to bring the wheel back onto the paved surface. There is no defined speed at which this is always safe as it will depend on many factors, including the size of the lip, the characteristics of the vehicle, and driver skill. However, most experts agree that the appropriate speed to remount the paved surface is 20 mph or less.

Right-of-Way Issues

Most State motor vehicle codes provide exceptions to standard right-of-way regulations for emergency vehicles responding to an emergency. However, drivers must realize that the safe implementation of these right-of-way waivers is dependent on the mutual recognition of the situation by both the driver of the emergency vehicle and the civilian motorist(s) in question. In other words, drivers must realize that they do not automatically have, **nor can they demand, the right-of-way**. By using warning devices that can gain the recognition of the civilian motorist(s), the driver is *requesting* the right-of-way. Actions such as ignoring approaching apparatus, refusing to yield, and driving erratically due to panic may be expected from the public. At all times, the driver must be prepared to yield the right-of-way in the interest of safety. One philosophy that is common is to drive as you would during nonemergency situations and take advantage of the room that clears for you on the road. While the number of right-of-way situations that may be encountered is almost endless, the two most common involve passing other vehicles and negotiating intersections (covered in the next section).

Safe passing of vehicles in order to gain the right-of-way is a situation that all fire apparatus drivers will encounter on nearly every emergency response. In general, it is best to avoid passing vehicles that are not pulling over to yield the right-of-way to the tanker. However, in some instances, the need to pass will occur, and the driver must be prepared to do it in the safest manner possible. The following guidelines should be used to ensure safe passing.

- Always travel on the innermost or left lane on multilane roads. Wait for vehicles in front of you to move to the right before proceeding.

- Avoid passing vehicles on their right sides **(Figure 4-28)**. Most civilian drivers' natural tendencies are to move to the right when an emergency vehicle is approaching. Thus, they could turn into your path if you are passing on the right. Some departments have strict SOP's prohibiting this practice. The exception to this would be in States that require vehicles to pull to the closest shoulder. In some cases, this may be the median, and passing those vehicles on their right side would be appropriate.

Figure 4-28 Never pass a vehicle on its right side.

- Make sure you can see that the opposing lanes of traffic are clear of oncoming traffic if you must move in that direction.

- Avoid passing other emergency vehicles if at all possible. However, in some cases, it may be desirable for a smaller, faster vehicle (such as an ambulance) to pass a larger, slower vehicle (such as a tanker). In these cases, the lead vehicle should slow down and move to the right to allow the other vehicle to pass. This maneuver should be coordinated by radio if possible.

Intersections

Statistics show that intersections are the most likely place for a crash involving all types of emergency vehicles. The case studies in this report do not appear to reflect that reality for tankers. However, this is probably a result of the fact that the cases studied here involved fatalities of firefighters. Intersection accidents involving tankers are most often not fatal to firefighters because more times than not, the vehicle the tanker strikes is considerably smaller than the tanker. In reality, intersections are just as dangerous for tankers as they are for any other emergency vehicle.

When approaching an intersection, the driver should slow the apparatus to a speed that allows a stop at the intersection if necessary. Even if faced with a green signal light, or no signal at all, the apparatus should be slowed to a speed that would allow for an expedient stop if necessary. Situations where an expedient stop may be required include if there are any obstructions, such as buildings or trucks, that block the driver's view of the intersection, or the driver cannot ensure that all other vehicles have stopped to give the tanker the right of way. At busy intersections, the driver should remove his or her foot from the throttle pedal and place it on the brake pedal so that there will be no delay if the need to stop occurs.

Depending on the motor vehicle statutes and departmental SOP's within a particular jurisdiction, tankers on an emergency response may proceed through a red traffic signal or stop sign after coming to a **complete** stop. Do not proceed into the intersection until you are certain that every other driver sees you and is allowing you to proceed. Simply slowing when approaching the intersection and then coasting through is not an acceptable substitute for coming to a complete stop. When proceeding through the intersection, attempt to make eye contact with each of the other drivers to ensure that they know you are there and about to proceed. This method is not foolproof. The only sure way is to visually ensure that all other vehicles have come to a complete stop.

Traffic waiting to make a left-hand turn may pull to the right or left, depending upon the driver. In situations where all lanes of traffic in the same direction as the responding apparatus are blocked, the apparatus driver should move the apparatus into the opposing lane of traffic and proceed through the intersection at an extremely reduced speed **(Figure 4-29)**. Oncoming traffic must be able to see the approaching apparatus. Full use of warning devices is essential. Driving in the oncoming lane is **not recommended** in situations where oncoming traffic is unable to see the apparatus, such as on a freeway underpass. Be alert for traffic that may enter from access roads and driveways. Approaching traffic on the crest of a hill, slow-moving traffic, and other emergency apparatus must be closely monitored.

Figure 4-29 In some cases it may be necessary to enter the opposing lane of traffic at an intersection.

The driver should also try to note if a green signal he or she is approaching has been in that position for a considerable amount of time. This could mean that it is ready to change to yellow at any moment. Anticipate this change and be prepared to stop if the change occurs as the apparatus nears the intersection. Another indicator of an impending signal change would be the pres ence of flashing "Do Not Walk" signs at pedestrian crossings. These lights typically begin flashing about 15 seconds or so before the green signal turns to yellow.

Some jurisdictions use traffic control or preemption devices to assist emer gency vehicles in negotiating intersections during their response. The driver must be aware of the traffic control devices used in his or her jurisdiction and how they operate. There are at least three different technologies that are used to help emergency vehicles gain control of traffic signals.

The most common preemption system, called an optical system, uses a spe cial strobe light called an emitter that is mounted to the fire apparatus and an optical receiver that is installed at the intersection. The emitter produces a flashing light at a precise frequency. When the receiver detects the presence of the flashing light, it sends an electronic request to the traffic signal controller to either prolong the green light for the approaching emergency vehicle or to cycle the intersection signal and provide the approaching emergency vehicle with a green light. These systems are capable of detecting the special strobe light at great distances, allowing time for pedestrians that may be in a cross- walk to complete their trip and for traffic approaching the intersection to stop and make way for the emergency vehicle to pass safely.

Some optical preemption systems provide a green light for the emergency vehicle only and display red lights to the other three directions of travel, and other systems give a green light to the emergency vehicle and to traffic travel ing in the opposing direction. In some jurisdictions, the traffic light standard may be equipped with a clear light that indicates to the tanker driver that the signal has been received and a green light is forthcoming. The tanker driver should not overly rely on this white light, as they have been known to fail at times due to mechanical or electrical problems. On some apparatus, the emit ter is wired into the parking brake system. When the parking brake is set, the emitter will be turned off. On apparatus that do not have this feature, the driver should remember to turn off the emitter when the apparatus is parked on the scene of an emergency. Otherwise, the emitter could affect any traffic signals that are within reach and disrupt the normal flow of traffic.

Another technology used for emergency vehicle preemption is a system that is activated by the emergency vehicle's siren as it approaches an intersection. A microphone on the traffic signal "hears" the siren and sends a signal to the traffic signal controller, ordering a preemption of the current traffic signal phase or a temporary hold on a green light that will allow the emergency vehicle to proceed. The microphone may be adjusted to order the preemption from dis tances of anywhere from a few hundred feet to about ½ mile. Intersections equipped with this system may have 3-inch clear and blue lights in each direc tion of travel, somewhere to the side of the regular traffic signals. As soon as the microphone sends the preemption signal to the signal controller, the direc tion of travel for the emergency vehicle gets a white light indicating that the signal was received and that a green traffic light is forthcoming. All other directions of travel get a blue light that indicates an emergency vehicle com ing from one of the other directions has gained control of the signal first. This is extremely important when emergency vehicles are approaching the intersection from more than one direction. Vehicles getting the blue light know that they will have to come to a stop because a green signal is not immediately forthcoming in their direction of travel.

The latest technologies in traffic preemption systems are those that use Global Positioning Systems (GPS) to activate traffic lights in favor of the responding apparatus. In these systems, the apparatus are equipped with GPS output devices that are tracked by satellite. Most GPS systems are able to track a moving apparatus accurately to within several yards of its actual position. It also will track the direction of travel and speed of apparatus. This information is relayed back to a monitoring system that determines which traffic lights the apparatus is approaching and changes the traffic light's signal to green (or keeps it green if it already was) to allow for safe passage of the apparatus.

Regardless of which type of traffic control devices are used in any jurisdiction, they are not substitutes for using proper defensive driving techniques. When traversing an intersection with a green signal, the driver must maintain a speed that will allow for evasive actions in the event another vehicle enters the intersection. If for any reason the fire apparatus does not get a green signal, the driver should bring the vehicle to a complete stop at a red signal. Keep in mind that if two apparatus equipped with signal control devices approach the same traffic signal from different directions, only the apparatus whose sensor affects the signal first will get a green light. The later-approaching apparatus gets a red signal. Do not assume that just because you did not get a green light that the system is not working. Approach the intersection with caution and come to a complete stop.

Rotaries/Roundabouts

Fire departments whose response districts include rotaries or roundabouts must include safe driving tactics for these intersections in their driver training program. Though the terms *rotary* and *roundabout* are often used interchangeably, in reality they are two different types of circular intersections. Circular intersections are those in which vehicles traverse by circulating around a center island, as opposed to crossing each other's path.

A *roundabout* is a circular intersection with yield control of all entering traffic, channelized approaches, counterclockwise circulation, and appropriate geometric curvature to ensure that travel speed within the intersection is less than 30 mph.

The term *rotary* (also called a traffic circle) is most commonly used in the eastern United States to describe older-style circular intersections that are missing one or more of the characteristics of a roundabout. Often, they have large diameters in excess of 100 yards and allow for speeds significantly greater than 30 mph.

Tankers must approach circular intersections with extreme caution. Most likely, the apparatus will have to yield to or completely stop for vehicles that are already within the intersection. When a safe opening becomes available, the tanker may enter the intersection using the designated direction of travel (almost always counterclockwise). No apparatus should ever be driven against the flow of traffic in a circular intersection. The apparatus should maintain a safe speed during the entire time it is in the intersection, and the driver should use the right turn signal when the tanker reaches the street it will be turning onto.

For more information on circular intersections, see the report by the U.S. Federal Highway Administration entitled *Roundabouts: An Informational Guide* (FHWA-RD-00-067) on the web at www.tfhrc.gov.

Railroad Crossings

Drivers must exercise caution when encountering railroad crossings during the emergency response. Crashes between fire apparatus and trains can be catastrophic events that result in serious injury or death to the firefighters on the apparatus. Much attention was focused on how fire apparatus should ne gotiate railroad crossings following a fatal collision in Catlett, Virginia, in 1989 (see the report at www.fema.usfa.gov/pdf/usfapubs/tr-048.pdf). These crashes are easily preventable as there is little mystery as to the route or direction a train is coming toward the apparatus.

In general, railroad crossings should be negotiated in much the same man ner as described above for intersections. In reality, a railroad crossing is just another type of intersection, albeit one that has the potential to place the tanker in the travel path of a moving vehicle that is significantly larger than the fire apparatus. When approaching a railroad crossing that has an acti vated signal, the driver should bring the tanker to a complete stop, even if there is no train passing at that time. Once the vehicle is stopped, the driver should look up and down the track in both directions to determine if there is a train approaching. If one is approaching, no effort should be made to cross the tracks. In some cases, a signal will be stuck in the "on" position. If no train can be seen for a significant distance, the tanker may proceed across the tracks. In other cases, a train may be parked close to the crossing and keeping the signal activated. Again, as long as the driver can ensure that there are no other moving trains approaching the crossing, the tanker may proceed across the tracks. If a parked train is blocking the driver's view, it may be necessary for one firefighter to exit the apparatus and cross the track(s) on foot to deter mine if it is safe for the apparatus to proceed.

Many railroad crossings in rural areas or industrial complexes are not equipped with active warning signals. A simple sign may note their location. In the case of crossings over private driveways there may be no marking what soever. Drivers should treat these crossings as though they have an activated warning light. The tanker should be brought to a complete stop and the track(s) visually checked for train traffic before proceeding across the crossing.

Valuable information on driver safety in relation to railroad crossings, as well as fire department operations in proximity to railroads, can be obtained from the national program entitled *Operation Lifesaver* (www.oli.org). This pro gram was originally developed in Idaho and quickly spread to other States. Eventually, it was operated by the National Safety Council. Since 1986 it has been a self-standing organization. Its mission is to educate drivers and pedes trians in making safe decisions around railroad crossings and tracks. Most of the information available from this organization can be applied to fire service situations.

Congested Areas

Tankers that are operated by fire departments located in suburban areas may at times need to be driven through areas that are congested with civilian mo tor vehicle traffic. These situations require the driver to exercise significant skill in handling the apparatus. The driver must remember that driving a large tanker in these conditions is much different than driving a smaller passenger vehicle. The tanker will not change lanes as easily as a smaller vehicle, and it will have a significantly longer stopping distance than smaller vehicles. At tempting to weave in and out of different lanes and following other vehicles too closely will likely place the tanker in a precarious situation.

Drivers who operate tankers, or any emergency vehicles for that matter, in congested traffic conditions must balance the urgency of their emergency re sponse with the patience necessary to maintain the vehicle safely under control at all times. In some cases it will be best to slow down and wait to take advan tage of openings that develop in the traffic. The driver cannot assume that all of the vehicles they are approaching will pull over and grant the tanker the right of way. In extremely congested areas, there may be nowhere for the other drivers to pull over. It may be necessary for a traffic signal to change or a similar action before the civilian vehicles can make room for the tanker to proceed. The driver of the tanker should never try to force his or her way through the congestion. This action increases the likelihood of a crash and may further increase the congestion problem.

The tanker may also need to be driven through areas that are congested with parked vehicles or other objects. Again, the driver should reduce the tanker's speed to one that allows the vehicle to negotiate the objects without striking them. If possible, have parked vehicles moved if it is necessary to ac cess a particularly tight location. It is generally quicker to move the obstruction than it is to spend a considerable amount of time going forward and back to get around it.

Areas of congestion should not be a surprise to the tanker driver. Through experience and preincident planning, the driver should be familiar with sec tions of the response district that tend to be problematic. The driver should also be knowledgeable about certain days of the week or times of the day that have a tendency to be more problematic than others. Rush hours in the morn ing and afternoon tend to increase traffic in business districts. Roads around malls and shopping centers tend to be busier on weekends and around holi days. All of these factors should be taken into account *before* going en route to an emergency. It may actually be more time efficient and safer to take a slightly longer, but less congested, route to the incident scene. Again, preincident plan ning will greatly aid these types of decisions.

High-Risk Areas

Within any jurisdiction there may be found one or more areas that pose a higher level of risk and require added judgment by the tanker driver. These areas may be permanent or temporary situations. Permanent high-risk areas include school and hospital zones. Temporary situations include fairs, carni vals, auctions, sidewalk sales, and yard/garage sales.

When approaching an active school zone during an emergency response, the driver must slow the vehicle to the speed indicated on the warning signs. Under no circumstances should the tanker be driven through the school zone faster than the posted speed limit. It is also advisable to curtail the use of audible warning devices in these areas as they may either frighten small children or cause them to run toward the street creating an additional hazard. The same principle should also be applied to hospital zones.

Temporary high-risk areas pose both vehicular and pedestrian hazards. They are often quite congested with parked vehicles, slow vehicles, and vehicles entering and exiting lanes of traffic. Pedestrians crossing the street between parked vehicles and from other dangerous locations compound this hazard. In the case of fairs, carnivals, and auctions, these events are typically planned and advertised in advance allowing the fire department to preincident plan and avoid these areas when possible. Sidewalk, yard, and garage sales may not be known to the fire department and will have to be dealt with by sound judgment when they are encountered. In most cases, treating these areas as was described above for school zones is a safe way of approaching the situation.

Backing the Apparatus

A significant portion of fire apparatus crashes occur while the apparatus is being driven in reverse. While these are rarely serious in terms or injury or death, they do account for a high percentage of fire apparatus crash repair costs. All fire departments should have firmly established procedures for backing the vehicle, and these procedures must always be followed by fire apparatus drivers. NFPA 1500 contains specific information on safe backing of the apparatus and should be consulted when developing a departmental backing policy.

As with most things in life, the easiest way to prevent a problem is to avoid the conditions that lead up to it. Whenever possible, the driver should avoid backing the fire apparatus. It is normally safer and sometimes quicker to drive around the block and start again. It is most desirable that new fire stations be designed with drive-through apparatus bays that negate the necessity to back the apparatus into them.

There are situations when it is necessary to back fire apparatus. This operation should be performed very carefully. When backing, there should be at least one firefighter -- and preferably two -- with a portable radio assigned to clear the way and to warn the driver of any obstacles obscured by blind spots **(Figure 4-30)**. If portable radios are not available, flashlights may be used at night to signal (but not blind) the driver. The department should establish preset signals for using the flashlights. If two spotters are used, only one should communicate with the driver. The second spotter should assist the first one. This is a very simple procedure that can prevent a large percentage of the crashes that occur during backing operations. Very simply, if you are the driver and you do

Figure 4-30 At least one of the guides should be equipped with a portable radio during backing operations.

Figure 4-31 Note the mirror next to the rear warning lights that allows the driver to view the backstep area of the apparatus.

not have or cannot see the spotters behind you, **do not back the apparatus!** All fire apparatus should be equipped with an alarm system that warns others when the apparatus is backing up.

There are several devices that may be attached to the apparatus to make backing operations safer. Some departments place a mirror at the rear of the apparatus that is visible through the driver's rearview mirror **(Figure 4-31)**. The second mirror is angled toward the rear step area of the vehicle and allows the driver to see if the end of the tailboard is approaching an object. Some apparatus are equipped with a camera that is mounted on the rear of the apparatus **(Figures 4-32 a & b)**. This camera transmits a significant view of the area behind the apparatus to a monitor in the cab. This allows the driver to view the rear of the apparatus while the apparatus is backing up. Both of these devices improve backing safety but neither are substitutes for having spotters assisting the driver during backing operations.

Some newer apparatus may be equipped with automatic sensing devices, often referred to as backstops, that will cause the vehicle's brakes to lock up and stop the apparatus when the device senses contact with an object. These devices are no substitute for having spotters assist with backing the apparatus. Backstop devices simply minimize the damage to the apparatus when it strikes an object. They do not prevent the crash. If the object being struck is a person, that person is still likely to be injured or killed.

Figure 4-32a A camera is mounted on the rear of the apparatus.

Figure 4-32b The monitor in the cab allows the driver to view the area behind the apparatus.

Staffing

While staffing may not appear to be an apparatus driving issue, in reality it is. In many jurisdictions, it is common for a fire department tanker to be operated by a lone driver. This is especially true of tankers that are equipped with automatic dump valves that can be operated without having to leave the apparatus cab. However, this report recommends that tankers being used to shuttle water be staffed by a minimum of two personnel (one driver and one passenger) at all times. The second person in the cab will act as a second set of eyes to monitor potential hazards as well as operate warning devices, check maps, and act as a spotter for backing operations when necessary. The second person can also assist with hose connections, portable tank deployment, and other necessary tasks on the emergency scene or at the fill site.

SAFE OPERATION OF FIRE TANKERS

If the tanker is going to be used as an attack apparatus, the staffing require ments contained in NFPA 1710, *Standard for the Organization and Deployment of Fire Suppression Operations, Emergency Medical Operations, and Special Operations to the Public by Career Fire Departments*; or NFPA 1720, *Standard for the Organiza-tion and Deployment of Fire Suppression Operations, Emergency Medical Operations, and Special Operations to the Public by Volunteer Fire Departments* should be fol lowed depending on whether the department is career or volunteer.

ONSCENE OPERATIONS

The majority of this document has focused on the safe operation of fire depart ment tankers during road travel. Certainly, most serious crashes or injuries and deaths involving the use of tankers occur during road travel. However, drivers of tankers also should be trained in positioning and operating the tanker in a safe manner while parked on an emergency scene. Drivers should keep in mind that their ultimate responsibility is the safety of the personnel assigned to the apparatus (as well as other personnel operating on the scene). Thus, while it is always desirable to locate the tanker in a position where it will not be subject to being hit by another vehicle, there are cases where the best op tion might be to use the tanker as a shield to protect firefighters from oncoming traffic. This section explores the various strategies that may be used to protect the apparatus and the personnel during onscene operations.

Because this document is focused primarily on safety issues, extensive infor mation on tactical positioning for tankers on the emergency scene will not be covered. Tactical positioning information can be obtained from most of the training manuals listed in the bibliography contained in **Appendix C** of this document.

Safely Positioning the Tanker

As mentioned above, the driver of a tanker has two primary options when determining where to park the apparatus on an emergency scene:

1. Park the apparatus in a manner that reduces the chance of the vehicle being struck by oncoming traffic.

2. Park the apparatus in a manner that shields firefighters and the opera tional work area from being exposed to oncoming traffic.

The procedures for performing each of these options will differ depending on the type of road and surroundings at which the emergency scene is located. Drivers must be versed in the appropriate positioning procedures for all of the possible environments that they may be expected to operate within.

SURFACE STREETS AND ROADS-

The term *surface streets and roads* refers to all thoroughfares that are not di vided or limited-access highways. They range from rural, unpaved roads to busy, urban and suburban avenues. As mentioned above, most often the tac tical needs of the incident will dictate the positioning of the tanker. If the tanker is to be used in a water shuttle operation, it will not really be positioned at all. At most, it will be staged until it can access the dump site to drop its load.

However, in many cases, the tanker will be used at a stationary location on the incident scene. This is particularly common in the case of pumper/tankers that are used as attack apparatus. In these situations, the tactical needs of the incident will dictate its position. However, there are some safety principles that should be followed as much as possible:

- Park the apparatus off the street in a parking lot or driveway. This may not be as easy with tankers as it is with other vehicles because of their large size. The driver needs to make sure that the parking lot or driveway is adequate enough to support the weight of the apparatus.

- Close the street that the emergency is located on to through traffic. This eliminates the potential of a civilian vehicle driving into the apparatus or firefighters.

- Do not park the apparatus within the collapse zone of a building involved in a structure fire. The collapse zone is commonly considered to be equal to one and one-half times the height of the building.

- Do not block access to the scene for later-arriving emergency vehicles. Oftentimes crashes occur when one vehicle is parked in a poor position and another attempts to squeeze around it.

- If the emergency scene is in the street, such as with a vehicle fire or motor vehicle crash, and the street may not be closed to all traffic, park the tanker in a manner that uses it as a shield between the scene and oncoming traffic. It would be better for a stray vehicle to drive into the fire apparatus than it would be for it to strike a group of responders (**Figure 4-33**).

Figure 4-33 The apparatus may be used to shield the scene. *Courtesy of IFSTA/Fire Protection Publications*

- On EMS calls, use the tanker to shield the patient loading area behind the ambulance (**Figure 4-34**). This area is particularly vulnerable to oncoming traffic.

- Never park the apparatus on railroad tracks. Keep the apparatus far enough away from the tracks so that a passing train will not strike it. Park the apparatus on the same side of the tracks as the incident. This negates the need to stretch hoselines across the tracks or for personnel to be traversing back and forth between each side.

The United States DOT publishes a document entitled *Manual on Uniform Traffic Control Devices* that provides excellent information for setting up and marking work zones. It also gives guidance on when and how to reroute traffic. The

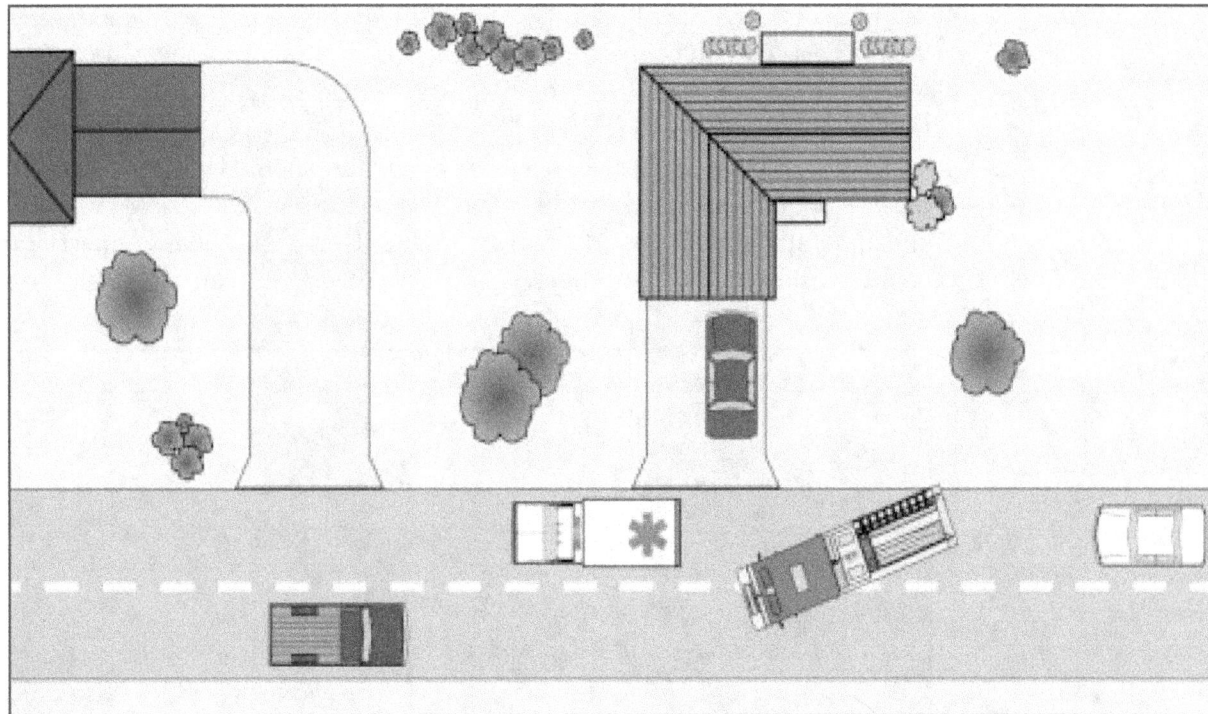

Figure 4-34 Shield the ambulance loading area with the tanker. *Courtesy of IFSTA/Fire Protection Publications*

information should be applied to emergency scenes whenever possible. It is an excellent source of reference for developing fire department SOP's/guidelines on incident scene safety.

LIMITED-ACCESS HIGHWAYS

Some of the most dangerous scenarios faced by firefighters are operations on highways, interstates, turnpikes, and other busy roadways. There are numerous challenges relative to apparatus placement, operational effectiveness, and responder safety when dealing with incidents on limited-access highways.

Simply accessing the emergency scene on a limited-access highway can be a challenge to emergency responders. Apparatus may have to respond over long distances between exits to reach an incident. In some cases, apparatus will be required to travel a long distance before there is a turnaround that allows them to get to the opposite side of the median. Apparatus should not be driven against the normal flow of traffic unless police units have closed the road.

The driver should use common sense when responding to an incident on a highway or turnpike. A fire apparatus usually travels slower than the normal flow of traffic, and the use of warning lights and sirens may create traffic conditions that actually slow the fire unit's response. Many fire departments have SOP's that require the driver to turn off all warning lights and audible warning devices when responding on limited-access highways. The warning lights are turned back on once the apparatus reaches the scene. However, as discussed earlier in the chapter, only select warning lights should be used to prevent the blinding of oncoming civilian drivers.

It is important that police and fire department personnel have a good working relationship and compatible SOP's when operating at highway incidents. At a minimum, at least one lane next to the incident lane should be closed **(Figure 4-35)**. Additional or all traffic lanes may have to be closed if the extra lane does not provide a safe barrier. Fire apparatus should be placed between the flow of traffic and the firefighters working on the incident to act as a shield. The apparatus should be parked on an angle so that the tailboard protects the operator from traffic. Front wheels should be turned away from the firefighters

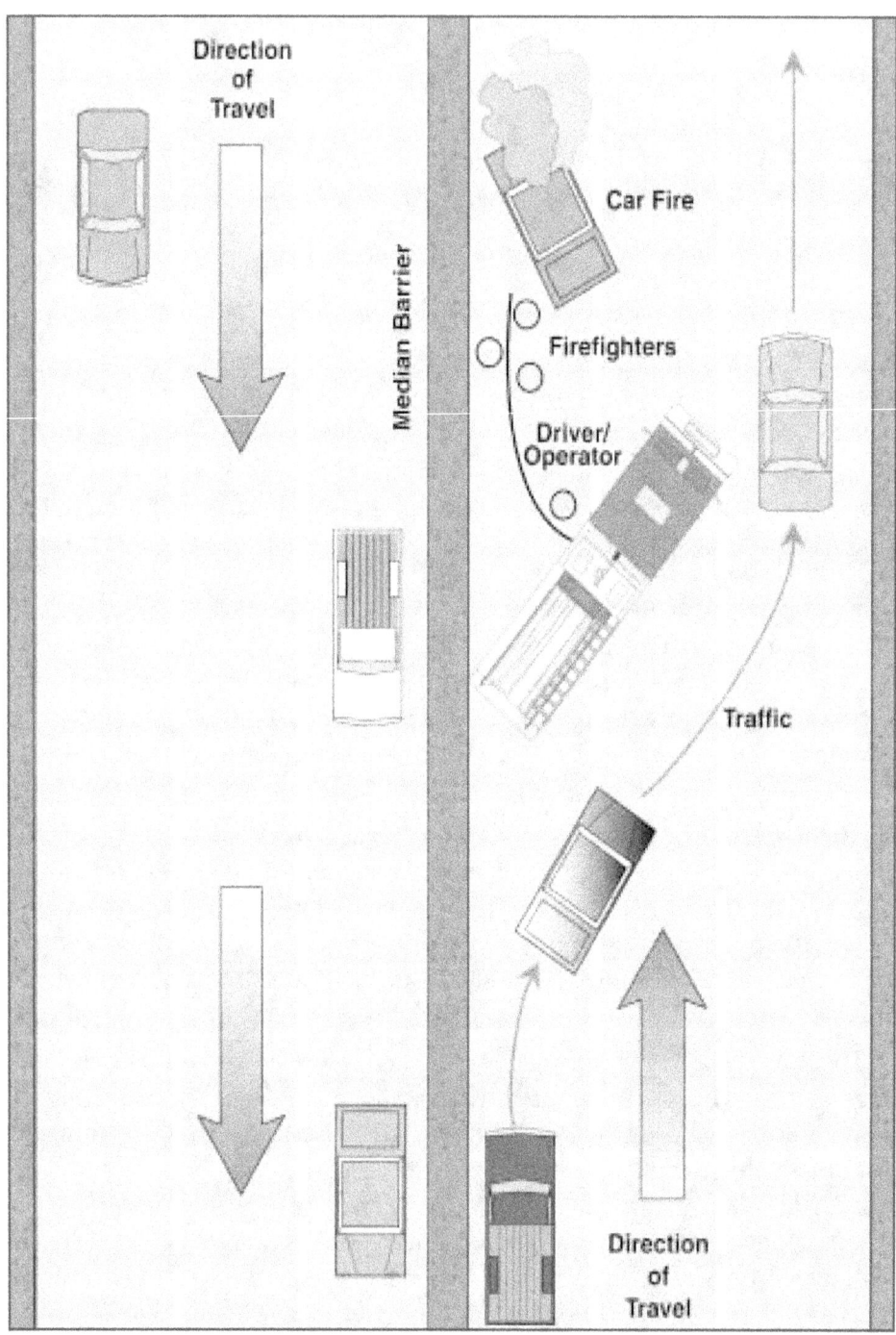

Figure 4-35 Attempt to close the lane next to the incident when operating on multilane highways. *Courtesy of IFSTA/Fire Protection Publications*

SAFE OPERATION OF FIRE TANKERS

working highway incidents so that the apparatus will not be driven into them if struck from behind. Also consider parking additional apparatus 150 to 200 feet behind the shielding apparatus to act as an additional barrier between firefighters and the flow of traffic.

All firefighters must use extreme caution when getting off the apparatus so that they are not struck by passing traffic. The firefighters should only mount and dismount the apparatus on the side opposite flowing traffic whenever possible. Similarly, drivers are extremely vulnerable to being struck by motorists if they step back beyond the protection offered by properly spotted apparatus.

At the time of this report, a significant amount of research and work on responder safety on highways was underway by organizations such as the U.S. Fire Administration (www.fema.gov/usfa), Cumberland Valley Volunteer Firemen's Association, and the Emergency Responder Safety Institute (www.respondersafety.com). Each of these sources can provide additional information on this topic.

Water Shuttle Operations

Water shuttle operations, sometimes referred to as tanker shuttles, are used to supply water to emergency scenes that are so remote from the water supply source that relay pumping is not practical. Water shuttles involve a process in which tankers deliver their load of water to the emergency scene (the dump site), travel to a filling site, reload with water, and then return to the emergency scene to dump again. Water shuttle operations are among the most common types of uses for fire department tankers.

Water shuttle operations involve a significant amount of maneuvering and driving on the part of the tanker driver. Most of the maneuvering occurs when the tanker is preparing to be filled or unloaded. Any measures that can be taken to reduce the amount of fine maneuvering that must be done at the fill or dump site will accordingly increase the level of safety at each location and will reduce the fill and dump times. Selecting an appropriate route of travel between the two sites also has an impact on safety. Because the first tanker driver or crew on the scene will often be responsible for establishing the fill and/or dump sites and the shuttle route of travel, it is important for tanker drivers to understand the selection of these sites and route. It is preferable that many of these decisions be made in preincident planning for target hazards and geographical areas within each jurisdiction. The preincident plan can contain the best fill site, alternative fill sites, the dump site, and desired route of travel for all shuttle apparatus.

Some jurisdictions have SOP's that limit the number of tankers that may be assigned to a single fill or dump site location to four or five tankers. In theory, this reduces congestion at the sites and the down time waiting to load and fill. This procedure may not work in all jurisdictions or situations. In particular, where there is a very long distance between the fill and dump sites, limiting the operation to four or five tankers may not ensure that a continuous supply of water is available at the dump site/scene. More tankers may need to be added in order to make up for the long haul distance.

Water shuttle operations must be integrated into the incident management structure. Mostly commonly, they will be assigned their own group or sector in the incident management system. The Water Supply Supervisor will be in charge of the overall shuttle operation. One individual each should be placed in charge of fill and dump sites. These people may be referred to as the Fill Site Manager and the Dump Site Manager.

DUMP SITE CONSIDERATIONS

The location of the dump site obviously should be in close proximity to the incident scene. However, the front and center of the incident may not al ways be the best location for the dump site. An example of this situation is when the fire scene is located down a narrow lane, driveway, or dead-end street. In these cases, it would be advantageous to locate the dump site at the intersection where the lane, driveway, or dead-end street meets a thor oughfare. The dump site pumper then relays water to the attack pumper located at the fire scene.

Even when the fire scene is located on a through street, early arriving appa ratus may block the front of the fire scene. Because they have committed hoselines or aerial devices, it is not practical to reposition the trucks to provide through access for a water shuttle. In this case, the dump site may be established at an intersection close to the scene, again with the dump site pumper supplying water to attack apparatus at the scene. Large parking lots near the fire scene also make excellent dump sites.

Figure 4-36 Side dumps require the least positioning of apparatus at the dump site.

Tanker drivers should use extreme caution when pull ing into the dump site. There tends to be a significant number of apparatus parked at this location and nu merous personnel moving around. The driver must anticipate the need to stop the apparatus in a short distance and should gauge his or her speed accordingly. Generally, it is best not to approach the portable water tanks until receiving a verbal or visual signal to do so.

Personnel at the dump site should assist the arriving tanker driver with positioning the apparatus so that the tank discharge is properly located to dump water into the portable tank **(Figure 4-36)**. The most efficient apparatus have tank discharges located on either side of the vehicle. This allows the tanker to simply be driven next to the tank and unloaded. Some tankers have their sole tank discharge located on the rear of the appara tus. This requires the tanker to be backed into the tank in order to dump its load. When this is the case, the proper procedures for safe backing of the apparatus described earlier in this chapter should be followed. It may also be possible to modify the rear discharge by constructing a chute that directs the water to one side or the other **(Figure 4-37)**.

Figure 4-37 Rear dumps may be modified to discharge to either side of the apparatus.

FILL SITE CONSIDERATIONS

Each fire department should have knowledge of appropriate fill sites in its jurisdiction before an incident occurs. Drivers and fire officers should have a good knowledge of all the water system hydrants, dry hydrants, and suitable drafting locations within their response district. When the need to establish a water shuttle occurs, the IC or water supply group/sector supervisor should select the closest suitable water supply source to the scene. Depending on the situation, the closest *suitable* water supply source may not necessarily be the actual closest water supply source. For reasons of travel safety or water flow requirements, it sometimes may be better to establish a fill site at a location that is somewhat farther from the dump site than the closest source.

When selecting a fill site, try to pick a location that requires a minimum of maneuvering or backing of tankers when they arrive at that location. This speeds the operation and lessens the chance of a crash. The best fill sites are those in which the tankers drive straight in from one direction, fill, and then proceed straight out the other end **(Figure 4-38)**. If some maneuvering of the apparatus is unavoidable, remember that it is always easier to maneuver apparatus before the tank is filled than after.

Figure 4-38 Fill and dump sites that allow the apparatus to drive straight in and out, without backing or maneuvering, are the most desirable.

If at all possible, locate the fill site at a location closed to civilian traffic. This lessens the chance of crashes occurring while tankers are being maneuvered. As described above for dump sites, the driver should approach and enter the fill site with caution and be prepared to stop immediately, if necessary.

SELECTING THE ROUTE OF TRAVEL

A key safety decision in setting up the water shuttle operation is establishing the route of travel for tankers going between the fill and dump sites. Driving the shuttle route is one of the most hazardous tasks for tanker drivers. The route of travel for the shuttle operation should take both safety and operational efficiency into consideration.

- A circular route of travel is considered to be the optimum method for conducting a water shuttle operation. When a circular pattern is employed, the full tankers leaving the fill site follow one route of travel toward the dump site. The empty tankers leave the dump site and proceed to the fill site using a different route of travel. This method eliminates the possibility of large trucks needing to pass each other on narrow, rural roads. This method also can be employed on incidents that occur on limited-access or divided highways.

- If possible, roadways used during shuttle operations should be closed to all traffic other than emergency vehicles. This is particularly important when it is not possible to use a circular shuttle pattern. In these cases, fire apparatus traveling back and forth on the same road will cause a lot of confusion for members of the public driving on the same road, and drivers in the shuttle must exercise additional caution.

PREVENTING FIRE DEPARTMENT TANKER CRASHES

A number of other safety issues must be considered when selecting a particular route of travel. These include the following:

- *Narrow roads.* The problems posed by these roads include difficulty passing other vehicles and the possibility of getting the apparatus tires off the road surface and causing a crash.

- *Long driveways.* These driveways often require tight maneuvering of the apparatus by the driver. Improper coordination also can result in apparatus approaching each other from opposite directions. At worst, this could result in a serious accident. At best, one of the rigs would be forced to back out all the way because of its inability to pass the other rigs.

- *Blind curves and intersections.* Vehicles may cross the centerline on blind curves and enter the path of another vehicle. Blind intersections pose an extreme danger when the driver cannot see oncoming cross traffic. The reverse may also be true when drivers of civilian vehicles cannot see oncoming apparatus. When possible, use police officers, fire police, or other qualified personnel to control the flow of traffic at dangerous intersections along the shuttle route.

- *Winding roads.* Winding roads require a lot of concentration on the part of the driver. One slight slip in attention level can result in a crash.

- *Steep grades.* Steep grades, both uphill and downhill, can cause problems for drivers. Uphill grades slow the shuttle operation and cause excessive wear on the vehicle. Driving on downhill grades also can be dangerous. Brake fade can result in the driver being unable to slow or stop the vehicle at the bottom of the hill.

- *Inclement weather conditions.* Roads that have not been cleared of ice, snow, standing water, mud, or storm debris should be avoided.

CONCLUSION

There are many actions that can be taken to reduce the incidence of fire department tanker crashes. These include better driver training programs, better apparatus design, proper maintenance programs, and responsible behavior on the part of the tanker driver. By following and implementing the information that was covered in this chapter, there is no doubt that the fire department will be successful in reducing the likelihood of a tanker crash within its department.

Tankers account for the largest number of firefighter crash deaths of all types of fire department vehicles. This figure becomes even more disproportionate when one considers that tankers account for only an estimated 3 percent of all fire apparatus in the United States. These facts signal the need to analyze the problem and take prudent corrective actions to avoid these situations in the future. This report is part of the United States Fire Administration's effort to begin corrective action in this regard.

This report has examined the various causal factors that have been identified as problematic for tankers and their drivers. Through statistical analysis we identified the most common of these causes. Case studies of fatal tanker crashes were reviewed for the purpose of learning from the mistakes that were made. Finally, an extensive overview of the training, technological, and programmatic means for preventing future tanker crashes was undertaken.

Although all of the information in this report is pertinent to the problem of tanker crashes and their prevention, certainly there are some factors that stand out as being especially crucial. Since the purpose of this report is to avoid these crashes in the future, there is no better way to end it than by restating the most important actions that can be implemented to reduce the frequency and severity of tanker crashes:

1. **Operate the tanker at a safe and reasonable speed.** Never drive the tanker faster than a speed at which it can be fully controlled. Never exceed the posted speed limit when driving under nonemergency response conditions.

2. **The cautionary speed signs that accompany road signs indicating curves in the road should be considered the maximum speed for a tanker driving on these curves in any condition.** In many cases, the suggested speed may be too high for tankers as they are developed for passenger cars on dry roads. It most cases, it will be necessary for the tanker to take the curve at a speed slower than what is posted.

3. **It is recommended that new tankers exceeding a GVWR of 32,000 pounds be equipped with antilock braking systems.** NFPA 1901 requires antilock brakes for all vehicles exceeding 36,000 pounds.

4. **Keep all of the wheels on the primary road surface at all times.** Having the tanker's right-side wheels drift off the edge of the road is one of the most common causes of tanker crashes. If the right-side wheels do get off the edge of the road, do not try to bring the apparatus back onto the road surface at a high speed. Slow the apparatus to 20 mph or less before trying to bring the wheels back onto the road surface.

5. **Travel with the water tank either completely empty or completely full.** This minimizes the effects of liquid surge within the tank. This is a good idea even if the tank is properly baffled, and it is crucial if the tank is not properly baffled.

6. **Avoid operating retrofit tankers if at all possible.** Every attempt should be made to place in service tankers that were specifically engineered and designed for fire department operations. Serious accidents have been attributed to poorly designed, retrofitted, or homebuilt tankers.

7. **Know the weight of your apparatus.** All tankers should be weighed completely full and that weight should be posted (in units of pounds and tons) on a plaque on the vehicle's dashboard. This will help the driver to determine if it is safe to drive the vehicle on a road or bridge that has posted weight restrictions.

8. **Require mandatory training for tanker drivers.** This must include extensive training before being allowed to drive the tanker on public roadways and refresher training on a regular basis according the requirements of NFPA 1451 and NFPA 1500.

9. **Establish an effective maintenance program for the tanker and all other fire department vehicles.** Many mechanical failures that lead to crashes can be prevented if the apparatus is inspected and maintained on a regular basis. Guidelines for establishing proper maintenance programs can be found in NFPA 1915. It is recommended that apparatus be inspected at least weekly.

10. **Use spotters when backing the apparatus.** Even though cameras and other devices for assisting with backing the apparatus do provide some measure of safety, there is no substitute for having at least one, preferably two, spotters to guide the driver while the apparatus is being operated in reverse. NFPA 1500 requires spotters for backing, regardless of whether the apparatus is equipped with cameras or other backing safety equipment. One spotter should be equipped with a portable radio in the event that they need to contact the driver during the backing operation.

11. **Retrofit all tankers with back-up alarms.** These devices warn other people in the area that a tanker is backing up. This will allow them to get out of the way before a crash occurs.

12. **Come to a complete stop at all intersections containing a stop sign or red traffic light in your direction of travel.** The most likely place to collide with another vehicle under emergency or nonemergency conditions is in an intersection. Nearly all of these crashes can be prevented if the tanker comes to a complete stop when faced with the signal to do so. The tanker may proceed through the intersection after assuring that all other vehicles have granted them the right of way to proceed. If the tanker driver cannot be certain that all vehicles are stopping to allow the tanker passage, the apparatus should not proceed.

13. **Wear your seatbelt whenever the apparatus is in motion.** While wearing a seatbelt may not prevent a crash from occurring, it certainly can minimize the risk to the driver (and the other occupants) in the event one does occur. A significant percentage of tanker accidents involves the vehicle rolling over and the driver and/or passenger(s) being thrown from the vehicle. The chance of serious injury or death is greatly multiplied when the occupant is thrown from the vehicle. Wearing of seatbelts will prevent nearly all ejections from the vehicle.

14. **Keep the windows rolled up.** This will add an extra measure of security in preventing the occupant(s) from being ejected from the apparatus in the event of a rollover crash.

15. **Be familiar with your response district and the roads within it.** By being familiar with the various routes within the response district, the driver will be able to anticipate when approaching hazardous sections of roads, dangerous curves, and other hazards to safe vehicle response.

16. **Avoid poorly constructed or unpaved roads whenever possible.** Again, familiarity with the response district will aid the driver in this objective. It may be safer (and faster) to take a paved route that is longer than the shorter unpaved route to an emergency scene.

17. **Limit the number of apparatus responding to an emergency to a reasonable, prudent number.** Dispatching three engines, two tankers, a heavy rescue squad, and three chief officers to a reported car fire on the interstate is overkill. The more vehicles that are on the road, the greater the odds of one of them being involved in a crash.

18. **Do not respond at an emergency rate (Code 3) when no emergency is known to exist.** Apparatus have been involved in collisions while re sponding with lights and sirens to perform a cover up at a neighboring station. This is not an emergency. As well, fourth or fifth due apparatus have been involved in crashes well after the initial apparatus arrived on the scene and found no fire or emergency condition. As soon as it is determined that no emergency exists, or that the initial arriving appa ratus can handle the emergency, all other responding apparatus should be directed to reduce their response to a nonemergency rate.

19. **Always have at least one firefighter accompany the driver of the tanker.** The passenger can assist by operating warning devices, han dling radio transmissions, and being a second set of eyes. The passenger should not hesitate to warn the driver when they feel that the tanker is being operated at an unsafe speed.

20. **Practice driving the tanker in adverse road conditions.** It is not rea sonable to expect that a driver who has only been trained in daylight hours, on clear dry roads will be qualified to operate the vehicle safely at night on in adverse weather.

CASE HISTORIES OF TANKER CRASHES INVOLVING FATALITIES -- 1990 TO 2001

The following is a compilation of all locatable incident reports on fire department tanker crashes involving firefighter fatalities during the period of 1990 through 2001.

CASE NUMBER 1

Date of Incident: May 7, 1990
Time of Incident: 10 p.m.
Location of Incident: Long Creek, Mississippi
Significant Causal/Severity Factors:

- Wheels left the right side of the road
- Overcorrection when attempting to bring right wheels back onto the road surface
- Failure to wear seatbelts

Number of Firefighter Fatalities: 1

The Incident:

The 70-year-old male firefighter who was fatally injured was the driver of a tanker responding to an intentionally set trash container fire. A second firefighter rode in the right-front seat of the apparatus. The driver had 17 years of fire department experience and was a regular driver of the tanker. Neither firefighter was wearing a seatbelt at the time of the incident.

As the apparatus exited a curve in the road and approached a railroad bridge, the tanker left the right side of the roadway. The driver apparently overcorrected and the rear end of the tanker came around in a counterclockwise motion causing the tanker to roll. The tanker rolled several times, left the opposite side of the roadway, fell into a 75-foot gorge, and landed on railroad tracks at the bottom.

A firefighter notified the railroad company and an approaching freight train was stopped before it could collide with the tanker. Other responding firefighters made access to the scene using a series of ground ladders and extricated the injured firefighters. Since removal back up to the roadway above was impossible with the available equipment, a train carried the injured firefighters to the nearest road crossing. The driver died instantly of massive head and chest trauma and was pronounced dead at the scene. The other firefighter recovered.

CASE NUMBER 2

Date of Incident: May 17, 1990
Time of Incident: 2:17 p.m.
Location of Incident: Cresson, Pennsylvania
Significant Causal/Severity Factors:

- Excessive speed
- Failure to wear seatbelts
- Fatally injured individuals ejected from the apparatus

Number of Firefighter Fatalities: 2

The Incident:

Two firefighters had been working at the fire station since early in the morning, making sandwiches for a fundraiser. At 2:17 p.m., a mutual-aid request was received for a tanker to respond to a vehicle collision to provide additional water on the scene of a large gasoline spill. The two firefighters responded in the department's 1,800-gallon tanker. A 62-year-old male (past chief, 45-year member) was the driver and a 77-year-old male (50-year member) rode in the right-front seat. Neither firefighter was wearing a seatbelt at the time of the incident.

As the apparatus descended a hill and entered a left-hand turn, the driver lost control of the tanker. The vehicle crossed over the centerline into the opposing lane, came back into the proper lane, and struck a guardrail on the right side of the road. The back end of the tanker came around against the guardrail and the apparatus began to roll. The tanker continued to roll and came to rest in a shallow creek bed off the right side of the road. Both firefighters were ejected as the tanker rolled. Both were killed instantly.

CASE NUMBER 3

Date of Incident: October 24, 1990
Time of Incident: 2 p.m.
Location of Incident: Spillway, Texas
Significant Causal/Severity Factors:

- Wheels left the right side of the road
- Overcorrection when attempting to bring right wheels back onto the road surface

Number of Firefighter Fatalities: 1 (also 1 civilian fatality)

The Incident:

A 26-year-old female firefighter was the driver of a 1,000-gallon tanker responding to a reported structure fire. The fire chief's 3-year-old daughter, who the driver was caring for at the time the fire was reported, was a passenger in the tanker.

While responding to the incident, the driver lost control of the truck, careened from side to side on the road for 650 feet, flipped over, and then crashed into a 20-foot ditch. The apparatus burst into flames when it came to a halt. The driver died of smoke inhalation and the child died of burns. Both were pronounced dead at the scene.

Fire department members reported that a blown tire had caused the driver to lose control of the vehicle but law enforcement members who investigated the collision found all of the tanker's tires to be intact. A state police investigator attributed the loss of control to the fact that the tanker left the right side of the pavement at the top of a hill. The water rolling from one side of the tank to the other caused the tanker to swerve from side to side until it left the roadway.

CASE NUMBER 4

Date of Incident: June 19, 1991
Time of Incident: 4:30 p.m.
Location of Incident: Blacksburg, Virginia
Significant Causal/Severity Factors:

- Wheels left the right side of the road
- Overcorrection when attempting to bring right wheels back onto the road surface
- Failure to wear seatbelts
- Fatally injured individual ejected from the apparatus

Number of Firefighter Fatalities: 1

The Incident:

The 30-year-old male firefighter (15-year veteran of the fire department) who was fatally injured was the driver of a 1,500-gallon tanker responding to the report of a fire in a manufactured home. A second firefighter was riding in the right-front seat. About one-quarter of a mile from the scene, the right wheels of the apparatus left the roadway. The driver steered the vehicle back onto the road but oversteered. The apparatus veered to the left and went off the roadway surface on the left. The driver again attempted to get control of the tanker and was steering to the right when the tanker overturned and ended up on its top.

The driver was not wearing a seatbelt and was ejected from the vehicle. The front seat passenger in the vehicle was wearing his seatbelt and was able to extricate himself from the tanker. Once free, he began to search for the driver. The driver was pronounced dead at the hospital 45 minutes after the collision.

CASE NUMBER 5

Date of Incident: June 19, 1991
Time of Incident: 4:30 p.m.
Location of Incident: Troy, Pennsylvania
Significant Causal/Severity Factors:
- Excessive speed
- Loss of control while descending a grade
- Failure to negotiate a left curve
- Failure to wear seatbelts
- Fatally injured individual ejected from the apparatus

Number of Firefighter Fatalities: 1

The Incident:

The 24-year-old male firefighter who was fatally injured was the driver of a tanker that had been moved up to another fire department's station while that department fought an arson fire in an illegal dump. After arriving at the fire station, the tanker was called to respond to the scene. A second firefighter was riding in the right-front seat. Neither firefighter was wearing a seatbelt at the time of the collision.

As the apparatus descended a hill during its response, it failed to negotiate a sharp left turn. The truck skidded off the road, struck a metal culvert pipe, went airborne for 24 feet, and then traveled for another 40 feet. The truck began to roll sideways down a hill and struck a tree. The driver was ejected and the tanker rolled over on top of him. The tanker continued to roll for another 12 feet and came to rest with the front wheels on the ground and the rear wheels at a 45-degree angle from the ground. The driver was pronounced dead at the scene. The firefighter who was the passenger received non-life-threatening injuries.

CASE NUMBER 6

Date of Incident: July 5, 1991
Time of Incident: 3:50 p.m.
Location of Incident: Hendersonville, Tennessee
Significant Causal/Severity Factors:
- Excessive speed
- Loss of control while descending a grade
- Failure to negotiate a left curve
- Failure to wear seatbelts
- Fatally injured individual ejected from the apparatus
- Wheels left the right side of the road

Number of Firefighter Fatalities: 1

The Incident:

The 20-year-old male firefighter who was fatally injured was the driver of a tanker that was responding to a grass fire with structural exposures threatened. The fire had originated in a trash-burning barrel. A second firefighter rode on the right-front seat of the tanker.

The fire chief and two pumpers were on the scene of the fire and the fire chief radioed responding units, including the tanker, to reduce their response to a nonemergency mode.

As the tanker descended a hill and entered a left curve, the apparatus ran off the right side of the road. The tanker struck a telephone pole before returning to the road. The rear of the truck came around and the apparatus rolled at least twice before coming to rest. The total distance traveled from the point at which the tanker left the road until it came to rest was 312 feet.

The driver was ejected from the tanker. Emergency medical assistance was provided at the scene and en route to the hospital. The driver was pronounced dead shortly after arriving at an emergency room. The firefighter who was the passenger received non-life-threatening injuries.

CASE NUMBER 7

Date of Incident: December 9, 1991
Time of Incident: 10:55 a.m.
Location of Incident: Biloxi, Mississippi
Significant Causal/Severity Factors:
- Wheels left the right side of the road
- Overcorrection when attempting to bring right wheels back onto the road surface

Number of Firefighter Fatalities: 1

The Incident:

The 20-year-old male firefighter who was fatally injured was the driver of a 1,600-gallon tanker that was returning to the fire station after fueling the apparatus at the county work center. The truck's water tank was also full.

As the tanker neared the fire station, it negotiated a sharp curve. After coming through the curve, the right wheels of the apparatus left the road. The driver steered the truck back onto the road, but the vehicle traveled into the oncoming lane. The driver steered again and the truck returned to the proper lane, but it continued to the right and went off the road again. The truck began to roll and flipped onto its left side. The driver was wearing a lap-type seatbelt but he received fatal head injuries.

CASE NUMBER 8

Date of Incident: June 19, 1992
Time of Incident: 11:14 p.m.
Location of Incident: Lightstreet, Pennsylvania
Significant Causal/Severity Factors:

- Driver inattention
- Wheels left the right side of the road

Number of Firefighter Fatalities: 1

The Incident:

The 63-year-old male firefighter (a 48-year member of the fire department) who was fatally injured was the driver of a 1,500-gallon tanker that was responding to a vehicle fire. A second firefighter was riding in the right-front seat of the tanker. Neither firefighter was wearing a seatbelt at the time of the collision.

As the tanker ascended a hill at a slow to moderate speed (25 to 35 mph), the driver attempted to activate the unit's warning lights. The driver's attention was drawn to the switches (located to the left and below the steering wheel) because he was having difficulty finding the switches. As he searched for the switches, the tanker drifted off the right side of the road.

The passenger in the tanker, who was donning his protective trousers at the time, looked up and saw that the tanker was approaching a telephone pole. The passenger alerted the driver but it was too late to avoid a collision. The tanker impacted the telephone pole in front of the right-front tire and sheared the pole off at the base. The tanker continued over a private driveway and began to tip as it climbed a sloped embankment. The tanker struck a stone and cement retaining wall and then turned over onto its side and then onto its roof.

The driver died of skull and neck fractures. The passenger received non-life-threatening injuries.

CASE NUMBER 9

Date of Incident: July 12, 1992
Time of Incident: 2:50 p.m.
Location of Incident: Potosi, Missouri
Significant Causal/Severity Factors:

- Failure to wear seatbelts
- Fatally injured individual ejected from the apparatus
- Wheels left the right side of the road

Number of Firefighter Fatalities: 1

The Incident:

The 22-year-old male firefighter (a 5-year member of the fire department) was responding as the lone occupant and driver of a 1,200-gallon tanker en route to a vehicle collision. The tanker's speed was estimated at between 50 and 55 miles per hour. The driver was not wearing a seatbelt at the time of the collision.

The right side wheels of the tanker left the roadway and the vehicle struck a culvert. The steering assembly was sheared off, and the rear axle was broken loose from the chassis. The tanker came back onto the roadway, turned sideways, and rolled three times. The driver was ejected from the vehicle and was thrown into a gully on the left side of the roadway.

CASE NUMBER 10

Date of Incident: December 1, 1992
Time of Incident: 1:15 p.m.
Location of Incident: Bryan, Texas
Significant Causal/Severity Factors:

- Excessive speed
- Loss of control while descending a grade
- Failure to negotiate a right curve
- Failure to wear seatbelts (disputed)
- Fatally injured individual partially ejected from the apparatus

Number of Firefighter Fatalities: 1

The Incident:

The 33-year-old female firefighter who was fatally injured was the driver of a 2,000-gallon tanker that was responding to a mutual-aid request for assistance at a 200-acre grass fire. A second firefighter was riding in the right-front seat. The law enforcement report on the incident does not indicate any seatbelt use by either firefighter; the fire department report maintains that lap belts were used by both firefighters.

The first mutual-aid apparatus arrived on the scene and ordered all other responding apparatus to discontinue their emergency response and continue to the scene in a nonemergency mode. The tanker involved in the collision acknowledged the order.

As the tanker approached the scene, it descended a steep hill with a bend in the road to the right. The tanker crossed the centerline and traveled for a short distance in the opposing lane. The driver steered right and the truck returned to the correct lane briefly and then traveled back into the opposing lane of traffic. The tanker continued through the opposing lane, went off the left side of the road, fell into a ditch, and then the rear of the tanker swung around as the vehicle flipped and came to rest on its wheels. The law enforcement report reflected a speed of 68 miles per hour when the tanker left the road.

The passenger was fully ejected and driver was partially ejected. The driver was pronounced dead at the scene.

CASE NUMBER 11

Date of Incident: January 2, 1993
Time of Incident: 3:01 p.m.
Location of Incident: Nicholasville, Kentucky
Significant Causal/Severity Factors:

- Wheels left the right side of the road
- Overcorrection when attempting to bring right wheels back onto the road surface

Number of Firefighter Fatalities: 2

The Incident:

A 37-year-old male fire chief was the driver of a 2,000-gallon tanker returning from a car fire in a garage. A 27-year-old male firefighter was a right-front-seat passenger in the vehicle. Both firefighters were wearing their seatbelts.

The vehicle drove off the right side of the roadway onto a grassy area of the shoulder. The tanker traveled on the shoulder for approximately 60 feet. The driver steered the truck left and back onto the roadway, but the rear end of the truck came around and the vehicle left the left side of the road. As the tanker began to overturn, the truck impacted a tree. The tanker then spun around and came to rest partially in the roadway on its right side. The impact of the roof of the apparatus with the tree crushed the cab and delivered fatal head injuries to both firefighters.

Other firefighters who had just returned to the station or were en route to the station responded to a radio report of a fire apparatus collision. First-arriving firefighters assessed both injured firefighters and then called for extrication equipment, ambulances, and air ambulances. Access to the injured firefighters was limited and both were extricated using hydraulic rescue tools.

CASE NUMBER 12

Date of Incident: April 2, 1994
Time of Incident: 8:10 p.m.
Location of Incident: Montevallo, Alabama
Significant Causal/Severity Factors:

- Loss of control while descending a grade
- Failure to wear seatbelts
- Fatally injured individual ejected from the apparatus
- Wheels left the right side of the road
- Overcorrection when attempting to bring right wheels back onto the road surface

Number of Firefighter Fatalities: 1

The Incident:

The 17-year-old male firefighter who was fatally injured was a right-front-seat passenger in a 1,200-gallon tanker responding to a report of a woods fire that was threatening to extend to structures. The route to the incident included a road with a number of curves and hills. According to the law enforcement report, seatbelts were not present in the vehicle.

As the tanker descended a hill, it left the right side of the roadway and traveled approximately 159 feet on the shoulder. The reflected lights of a car following the tanker in the tanker's mirrors may have blinded the tanker driver. The driver steered the truck to the left and back onto the road surface but was then faced with another sharp curve to the right. As the driver turned the wheel to the right to negotiate the curve, the right side of the apparatus came around and the truck began to roll. The tanker left the roadway and struck a tree, finally coming to rest on its wheels.

When the vehicle came to rest, the passenger was thrown halfway out the rear window opening on the driver's side of the apparatus. The driver of the tanker did not suffer any major injuries and was able to provide care to the firefighter. The firefighter was extricated by other firefighters and pronounced dead at the scene by the coroner. The cause of death was listed as head and chest trauma.

CASE NUMBER 13

Date of Incident: August 8, 1994
Time of Incident: Not reported
Location of Incident: California
Significant Causal/Severity Factors:

- Unknown

Number of Firefighter Fatalities: 1

The Incident:

A male wildland firefighter for the United States Forestry Service was killed in this collision. No additional information was available for this incident.

CASE NUMBER 14

Date of Incident: September 22, 1994
Time of Incident: 7 p.m.
Location of Incident: Livingston, Texas
Significant Causal/Severity Factors:

- Excessive speed
- Failure to wear seatbelts
- Fatally injured individual ejected from the apparatus
- Possible impairment by prescription medication(s)

Number of Firefighter Fatalities: 1

The Incident:

The 41-year-old captain was responding to a kitchen fire as the driver and sole occupant of a 3,000-gallon tanker. He was not wearing a seatbelt at the time of the collision.

As the apparatus attempted to make a right-hand turn onto a main road, the vehicle failed to negotiate the turn and rolled twice. The driver was ejected from the vehicle and was pronounced dead at the scene. Cause of death was listed as multiple traumatic injuries. Law enforcement reports cited unsafe speed (though under the posted speed limit) as a factor in the rollover. There was also some indication that the driver may have been taking prescription medication that impaired his judgment at the time of the collision.

CASE NUMBER 15

Date of Incident: December 29, 1994
Time of Incident: 4:28 p.m.
Location of Incident: Melfa, Virginia
Significant Causal/Severity Factors:

- Excessive speed
- Failure to negotiate a curve
- Failure to wear seatbelts

Number of Firefighter Fatalities: 1

The Incident:

The 18-year-old firefighter who was fatally injured was the driver of a 2,000-gallon tanker responding to the report of a structure fire in a poultry house. Another firefighter rode as a passenger in the right-front seat. Both the driver and the passenger were wearing seatbelts.

After the apparatus negotiated a curve, the driver lost control of the vehicle, and the tanker went off the left side of the road. The tanker struck two trees before it became airborne, struck another tree, and rolled two to four times. The driver was killed due to a dislocated cervical spine; the other firefighter was severely injured but survived. The police report cited excessive speed as a factor in the collision. The reported structure fire turned out to be a controlled burn.

CASE NUMBER 16

Date of Incident: April 17, 1995
Time of Incident: 3:34 a.m.
Location of Incident: Castella, California
Significant Causal/Severity Factors:

- Excessive speed
- Loss of control while descending a grade
- Failure to negotiate a left curve
- Failure to wear seatbelts

Number of Firefighter Fatalities: 2

The Incident:

A 50-year-old female driver/operator lost control of a 1,000-gallon tanker while responding to a barn fire in an unfamiliar location. A 47-year-old male firefighter was also riding in the right-front seat. Neither was wearing a seatbelt at the time of the collision.

After receiving directions from a local citizen at the roadside, the driver/operator made a wrong turn and eventually descended a steep ½-mile hill. At the bottom of the hill, the tanker failed to negotiate a sharp left turn, struck a bridge guardrail, and either went through the guardrail or rolled over the top of it. The tanker fell into a rain-swollen creek below.

After all other fire department units had returned to the station from the dispatched barn fire, the absence of the tanker and two firefighters was noted. Firefighters fanned out to search for the missing tanker. The tanker was found upside down in the creek about 2-½ hours after the original dispatch.

Both firefighters were found deceased inside the cab of the apparatus. The cause of death for the passenger was listed as drowning and the cause of death for the driver/operator was listed as exposure and hypothermia.

CASE NUMBER 17

Date of Incident: May 12, 1995
Time of Incident: 2:40 p.m.
Location of Incident: Jacksonville, Arkansas
Significant Causal/Severity Factors:

- Overcorrection when attempting to bring right wheels back onto the road surface
- Poor road conditions

Number of Firefighter Fatalities: 1

The Incident:

The 22-year-old female firefighter who was fatally injured was the front right-seat passenger in a 1,000-gallon tanker that was engaged in driver training. Both the driver and firefighter were wearing lap-type seatbelts.

As the tanker proceeded on a small local road, the asphalt on the right side of the road crumbled. The driver of the tanker oversteered in an attempt to recover control, and the apparatus left the roadway on the left side of the road and struck a driveway culvert. The apparatus vaulted slightly and began to rotate. The vehicle rolled and came to rest upside down, partially in the roadway.

The passenger received fatal traumatic injuries; the driver of the apparatus was injured but his injuries were not life-threatening.

CASE NUMBER 18

Date of Incident: July 30, 1995
Time of Incident: 10:30 a.m.
Location of Incident: Aberdeen, Mississippi
Significant Causal/Severity Factors:

- Excessive speed
- Failure to wear seatbelts
- Fatally injured individual ejected from the apparatus
- Wheels left the right side of the road
- Overcorrection when attempting to bring right wheels back onto the road surface

Number of Firefighter Fatalities: 1

The Incident:

The 29-year-old male fire chief was the driver and sole occupant of a water tanker responding to a mutual-aid request for assistance at a barn fire. He was not wearing a seatbelt at the time of the collision.

A witness who was following the tanker reported that the apparatus was proceeding at an estimated speed of 65 miles per hour. The vehicle was seen to go off the right side of the roadway, come back onto the road, then roll over at least three times. The driver was ejected from the vehicle during the rollover.

A nurse who came upon the scene started CPR. Medical care was continued on the way to the hospital, but the driver was pronounced dead shortly after his arrival there. The cause of death was listed as internal injuries.

CASE NUMBER 19

Date of Incident: January 14, 1995
Time of Incident: 5:20 p.m.
Location of Incident: Salisbury, North Carolina
Significant Causal/Severity Factors:

- Excessive speed
- Failure to wear seatbelts
- Wheels left the right side of the road
- Overcorrection when attempting to bring right wheels back onto the road surface

Number of Firefighter Fatalities: 1

The Incident:

The 49-year-old male captain was the driver of a tanker responding to a report of a smoke odor in a manufactured home. A firefighter rode as the front seat passenger in the vehicle. Neither firefighter was wearing a seatbelt at the time of the collision.

Members of the first fire apparatus unit to arrive on the scene of the reported fire were told by other firefighters who had responded directly to the scene in their personal vehicles that there was no emergency. The operator of the first unit informed other responding units by radio to reduce their response mode to nonemergency. Firefighters standing near the truck heard the sound of the tanker collision at approximately the same time as this transmission was being made.

It was determined that as the unit responded, the right wheels of the tanker left the roadway. The driver steered the truck back onto the pavement, but the rear end of the tanker came around and the apparatus began to slide. The tanker left the left side of the road, rolled, and collided with a natural gas distribution substation.

A second tanker following the one that crashed alerted other firefighters to the collision. When firefighters arrived on the scene, they found the tanker entangled in the natural gas substation with large amounts of natural gas being released. A hazardous materials response team from a nearby city was called to the scene. Once the team arrived, the two occupants were removed from the tanker and transported to the hospital. The driver was pronounced dead at the hospital; the firefighter received serious but non-life-threatening injuries.

The cause of death for the driver was listed as multiple blunt force injuries to the head, chest, and abdomen. The law enforcement report on this incident cited speeding as a contributing circumstance to the collision.

CASE NUMBER 20

Date of Incident: April 8, 1996
Time of Incident: 9:36 p.m.
Location of Incident: Moses Lake, Washington
Significant Causal/Severity Factors:

- Excessive speed
- Failure to negotiate a curve
- Failure to wear seatbelts
- Failure to followed posted speed recommendations on a curve

Number of Firefighter Fatalities: 1

The Incident:

The 19-year-old male firefighter who was fatally injured was the driver of a 3,000-gallon tanker responding to a structure fire. The right-front seat was occupied by another firefighter. Neither firefighter was wearing a seatbelt at the time of the collision.

A local bridge was out of service for repairs, so the response route taken to the fire was unfamiliar to both firefighters. The fire chief, who was following the tanker in his vehicle, was more familiar with the route. As the tanker approached a curve, the fire chief realized that the driver was accelerating and ordered the tanker, by radio, to slow down. The order came too late, and the tanker entered the curve at a speed estimated to be 40 to 60 miles per hour. The posted recommended speed in the curve is 35 miles per hour.

The tanker skidded, rotated counterclockwise, and then left the right side of the roadway. The tanker rolled first onto its right side, then onto its roof. The cab was crushed as it slid for a distance, and the tanker rolled again and came to rest on its left side.

The fire chief and another chief officer who was riding with him immediately requested assistance. They found the passenger attempting to self-extricate and helped him out of the vehicle. They had a great deal of difficulty removing the driver due to his position in the cab of the truck. He was eventually removed with the assistance of a passing motorist. CPR was begun immediately and continued while the driver was transported to the hospital. The driver was pronounced dead shortly after his arrival at the hospital. The cause of death was listed as a lacerated heart and major vessels.

CASE NUMBER 21

Date of Incident: April 26, 1996
Time of Incident: 1 p.m.
Location of Incident: Beebe, Arkansas
Significant Causal/Severity Factors:

- Failure to negotiate a left curve

- Failure to wear seatbelts

- Fatally injured individual ejected from the apparatus

- Wheels left the right side of the road

- Overcorrection when attempting to bring right wheels back onto the road surface

Number of Firefighter Fatalities: 1

The Incident:

The 53-year-old male firefighter was the driver and sole occupant of a 1,200-gallon tanker responding to a structural fire. The driver was not wearing a seatbelt at the time of the collision.

As the tanker entered a left curve in the road, it went slightly off the right edge of the road. The driver overcorrected to the left, and the apparatus entered the oncoming lane of traffic. The driver steered right to bring the truck back into the proper lane but began to lose control. The tanker reentered the oncoming lane of traffic, rolled several times, and came to rest just off the right side of the roadway. The total distance traveled from the first corrective turn to the left to the final resting place of the apparatus was 223 feet. The driver was ejected from the vehicle, and his body was found approximately 53 feet from the final resting place of the tanker.

CASE NUMBER 22

Date of Incident: May 25, 1997
Time of Incident: 1:22 p.m.
Location of Incident: Jacksboro, Tennessee
Significant Causal/Severity Factors:

- Mechanical failure (brakes)

Number of Firefighter Fatalities: 1

The Incident:

The 41-year-old male firefighter who was fatally injured was the front right-seat passenger in a tanker that was responding to a collision with fire on a local highway. Neither the driver nor the passenger was wearing a seatbelt at the time of the collision.

As the apparatus approached an intersection, the driver attempted to slow the vehicle but the brakes failed. The tanker proceeded through the intersection at a speed later estimated to be 30 miles per hour.

On the other side of the intersection, in the tanker's path, a child was playing in the road. In order to avoid hitting the child, the driver was forced to swerve left. The tanker exited the left side of the roadway and began to roll onto its right side after coming into contact with a power pole guide wire. The tanker then slid and rolled to the other side of the roadway, struck another power pole, and came to rest on its roof. The passenger was ejected when the tanker collided with the guide wire. The tanker crushed the firefighter's head as it rolled.

An inspection of the tanker's braking system after the collision found a hole in a brake line near the rear axle differential.

CASE NUMBER 23

Date of Incident: July 9, 1997
Time of Incident: 6:24 p.m.
Location of Incident: Sandia, Texas
Significant Causal/Severity Factors:

- Excessive speed
- Failure to wear seatbelts
- Fatally injured individual ejected from the apparatus
- Wheels left the right side of the road
- Overcorrection when attempting to bring right wheels back onto the road surface

Number of Firefighter Fatalities: 1

The Incident:

The 54-year-old male firefighter was the driver and sole occupant of a 1,000-gallon pumper/tanker responding to a grass fire. The driver was not wearing a seatbelt at the time of the collision.

As the pumper/tanker approached another fire truck, the driver applied the brakes and skidded 58 feet. The right wheels of the pumper/tanker left the roadway and produced approximately 91 feet of skid marks on the right shoulder. The driver steered left, leaving 27 feet of right wheel skid on the pavement. The rear end of the truck came around in a counterclockwise direction, and the pumper/tanker began to roll.

The pumper/tanker crossed the centerline of the roadway and rolled into the opposing lane, the water tank separated from the truck, and the chassis continued into the ditch on the left side of the road. The driver was ejected during the process and was transported to a local hospital where he was pronounced dead. The cause of death was severe head injuries.

CASE NUMBER 24

Date of Incident: November 5, 1997
Time of Incident: 2:25 p.m.
Location of Incident: Danville, Virginia
Significant Causal/Severity Factors:

- Excessive speed
- Failure to negotiate a curve
- Failure to wear seatbelts
- Fatally injured individual ejected from the apparatus
- Wheels left the right side of the road
- Overcorrection when attempting to bring right wheels back onto the road surface
- Poor apparatus design (improperly baffled water tank)

Number of Firefighter Fatalities: 1

The Incident:

The 30-year-old male firefighter who was fatally injured was a passenger in a 1,000-gallon tanker that responded to the scene of a mutual-aid structure fire. Upon arrival at the scene, the initial driver/operator was ordered to perform other tasks, and the passenger became the driver/operator of the tanker. Water from the tanker was unloaded at the fire scene, and the tanker left the scene to refill at a nearby fire hydrant. A third firefighter accompanied the new driver to the fill site. Neither firefighter was wearing a seatbelt at the time of the collision.

After the tanker had been refilled, the tanker headed back to the fire scene. As the apparatus exited a curve, the right wheels left the roadway and ran onto the shoulder. The driver/operator overcorrected to the left, which brought the apparatus briefly into the oncoming lane of traffic. The driver/operator corrected again to the right, and the rear of the apparatus began to slide around. The tanker continued to slide and began to roll at some point. The vehicle came to rest on its roof, off the right side of the road.

Both firefighters were ejected from the tanker at some point in the rollover. The driver/operator received fatal traumatic injuries, and the other firefighter survived his injuries.

While at first glance this incident involves failure to keep the apparatus on the roadway, the investigation revealed that the water tank was only baffled to prevent forward and backward motion of the load. It did not have baffles to prevent sideward sloshing. It is believed that this accentuated the difficulty in regaining control of the vehicle once it began to slide sideways.

CASE NUMBER 25

Date of Incident: December 17, 1997
Time of Incident: 3:40 a.m.
Location of Incident: Cleveland, Tennessee
Significant Causal/Severity Factors:

- Wheels left the right side of the road

Number of Firefighter Fatalities: 1

The Incident:

The 33-year-old male firefighter who was fatally injured was the driver of a 1,250-gallon tanker that was responding without lights and siren to a field fire. A second firefighter was occupying the right-front seat. Both were wearing seatbelts.

During the response, the right wheels of the tanker left the right side of the road and went into a ditch. After striking a driveway culvert, the tanker came back onto the roadway and swerved right into an embankment. The tanker turned over and the cab was crushed all the way down to the doors. The distance from the point at which the tanker left the roadway to its final resting place was 362 feet. The driver was crushed and died of asphyxiation. The passenger survived the incident.

The field fire report ended up to be a boat that had been brought into a field and burned. The owner of the boat and an accomplice were charged with arson and other crimes.

CASE NUMBER 26

Date of Incident: May 5, 1998
Time of Incident: 5:45 p.m.
Location of Incident: Colorado City, Texas
Significant Causal/Severity Factors:

- Excessive speed
- Failure to wear seatbelts
- Fatally injured individual ejected from the apparatus
- Wheels left the right side of the road

Number of Firefighter Fatalities: 1

The Incident:

The 72-year-old male firefighter (50-year veteran) who was fatally injured was the driver of a 1,000-gallon converted tanker that was responding from one brush fire to another. A second firefighter was riding in the right-front seat. Neither firefighter was wearing a seatbelt at the time of the collision.

As the tanker crossed a narrow bridge, the driver yielded to the right to allow a vehicle headed in the opposite direction to pass. The right rear wheels of the tanker struck a concrete bridge support, and the driver lost control of the apparatus. The tanker rolled three times, ejecting both firefighters. The force of the collision broke the water tank from its mounts, and it separated from the tanker.

The driver was pronounced dead at the scene, and the other firefighter was transported to the hospital.

CASE NUMBER 27

Date of Incident: August 31, 1999
Time of Incident: 4:47 p.m.
Location of Incident: Center Rock, South Carolina
Significant Causal/Severity Factors:

- Excessive speed
- Failure to negotiate a curve
- Failure to wear seatbelts
- Fatally injured individual ejected from the apparatus
- Wheels left the right side of the road
- Overcorrection when attempting to bring right wheels back onto the road surface

Number of Firefighter Fatalities: 1

The Incident:

The 34-year-old male firefighter who was fatally injured was the driver of a 1,000-gallon pumper/tanker responding to a motor vehicle collision. A lieutenant rode in the right-front seat, and a firefighter was seated in the jump seat behind the driver. None of the three firefighters aboard the pumper/tanker was wearing seatbelts at the time of the collision.

As the apparatus responded around a curve in the road, it encountered a service truck headed in the opposite direction. The pumper/tanker's speed was estimated at 55 miles per hour in a 35-mile-per-hour zone. The pumper/tanker pulled to the right to accommodate the service truck, and the right wheels of the pumper/tanker left the roadway. The pumper/tanker traveled approximately 169 feet before the driver steered the apparatus back onto the road. The driver overcompensated or oversteered and the pumper/tanker crossed into the oncoming lane of traffic. The apparatus left the left side of the roadway, crossed through a yard, and traveled through a small ditch. The apparatus rolled once, became airborne, crossed another road, rolled again, and came to rest on its roof in a field.

The fire chief had been responding to the fire station but turned around to follow the pumper/tanker to the call. He lost sight of the pumper/tanker as it entered the curve and was alerted to the collision by a witness as he rounded the curve. The fire chief left his vehicle, encountered the injured lieutenant and firefighter, and was directed by those firefighters to the driver's location. The fire chief found no sign of life in the driver, who was trapped in the pumper/tanker. The driver was later extricated by other firefighters.

The lieutenant and firefighter received serious injuries but they recovered. The cause of death for the driver was listed as traumatic head injuries.

CASE NUMBER 28

Date of Incident: October 7, 1999
Time of Incident: 10:13 p.m.
Location of Incident: Pollock, Louisiana
Significant Causal/Severity Factors:

- Failure to negotiate a curve
- Failure to wear seatbelts
- Wheels left the right side of the road
- Overcorrection when attempting to bring right wheels back onto the road surface

Number of Firefighter Fatalities: 1

The Incident:

The 49-year-old male firefighter was the driver and sole occupant of a 3,000-gallon tanker responding to a mutual-aid structure fire. The driver was not wearing a seatbelt at the time of the accident. The road conditions were wet, and it was raining.

As the driver negotiated a curve, the right wheels of the tanker left the pavement on the right side of the road. The tanker traveled on the shoulder for approximately 98 feet. The driver steered left to bring the truck back onto the road, but the rear of the apparatus came around counterclockwise and the tanker began to roll. The tanker rolled and slid for approximately 57 feet and came to rest in the center of the road.

An EMS unit en route to the fire came upon the scene and discovered the driver still inside the vehicle with no vital signs. ALS procedures were administered at the scene and en route to the hospital. The driver was pronounced dead in the emergency room. The cause of death was listed as massive internal injuries, fracture of C-3, and transection of the spinal cord.

CASE NUMBER 29

Date of Incident: October 18, 1999
Time of Incident: 1:54 p.m.
Location of Incident: LaPorte, Indiana
Significant Causal/Severity Factors:

- Excessive speed
- Failure to negotiate a curve
- Failure to wear seatbelts (one victim)
- Fatally injured individual ejected from the apparatus (one victim)
- Failure to follow posted speed recommendations on a curve

Number of Firefighter Fatalities: 2

The Incident:

The 23-year-old male driver and 57-year-old male captain were responding in a 2,000-gallon tanker to a mutual-aid brush fire. The driver was not wearing a seatbelt at the time of the collision; however, the captain was properly belted.

The tanker failed to negotiate a curve in the road. The apparatus left the right side of the road and crossed into a cornfield, where it rolled several times. The speed of the tanker was estimated at 55 miles per hour. A caution sign before the curve recommended a maximum speed of 40 miles per hour. The driver was ejected from the vehicle, and the vehicle rolled on top of him. The captain was trapped in the tanker, which was on its roof, until he was extricated by other firefighters.

The captain died on November 4, 1999. He had been released from the intensive care unit to a regular hospital floor. The captain was seemingly well and recovering from his injuries. He was discovered pulseless and non-responsive; emergency care was provided but was not successful. The autopsy concluded that the captain died of a cardiac arrhythmia.

The driver died on January 22, 2000. He was making a slow recovery. The cause of death was listed as sepsis.

CASE NUMBER 30

Date of Incident: November 14, 1999
Time of Incident: 4:45 p.m.
Location of Incident: Richmond, Texas
Significant Causal/Severity Factors:
- Excessive speed
- Failure to negotiate a curve
- Failure to wear seatbelts
- Fatally injured individual ejected from the apparatus
- Wheels left the right side of the road
- Overcorrection when attempting to bring right wheels back onto the road surface
- Failure to follow posted speed recommendations on a curve

Number of Firefighter Fatalities: 1

The Incident:

The 46-year-old male firefighter was the driver and lone occupant of a 1,180-gallon tanker that was responding to a fire involving 200 round bales of hay that were near a home and a propane tank. The driver was not wearing a seatbelt at the time of the collision.

The tanker entered a curve at a speed above the posted limit. It was hugging the centerline and drove off the right side of the road as it completed the curve. The driver steered the truck left in an attempt to bring it back on to the road, but he oversteered and lost control. The driver locked up the tanker's brakes, and the tanker crossed the centerline and dug into the soft shoulder on the right side of the road. The truck rolled and came to rest upside down in a field. The driver was partially ejected and was trapped under the truck between the cab and the ground.

Firefighters arrived and extricated the driver with the use of airbags and hydraulic rescue tools. The extrication took about 40 minutes. The driver was pronounced dead at the hospital. The cause of death was listed as fractured ribs and sternum (flail chest).

Two 14-year-old boys were arrested, and one was charged with second-degree arson for setting the fire. As a part of a plea bargain, the boy was placed on probation until he turns 18.

CASE NUMBER 31

Date of Incident: December 15, 1999
Time of Incident: 1:30 p.m.
Location of Incident: Zwolle, Louisiana
Significant Causal/Severity Factors:

- Excessive speed
- Failure to negotiate a left curve
- Failure to wear seatbelts
- Fatally injured individual ejected from the apparatus
- Wheels left the right side of the road
- Overcorrection when attempting to bring right wheels back onto the road surface

Number of Firefighter Fatalities: 1

The Incident:

The 28-year-old male firefighter was the sole occupant and driver of a 1,500-gallon tanker responding to a report of a brush fire. The driver was not wearing a seatbelt at the time of the collision.

The radio in the tanker was off, so the driver did not hear a message from the dispatcher canceling the call and ordering responding units to return to quarters. As the tanker completed a left curve in the road, the right wheels of the tanker left the paved roadway and went onto a substandard shoulder. The driver attempted to steer the truck back onto the road, but the tanker began to rotate counterclockwise. The tanker then rolled over, ejecting the driver. The tanker came to rest in the middle of the road, and the driver landed off the left side of the road. From the point at which he was ejected to his final resting place, the driver traveled 141 feet.

The driver was pronounced dead at the scene. The cause of death was listed as multiple trauma. Careless operation of the vehicle was cited as a factor related to the collision in the law enforcement report.

CASE NUMBER 32

Date of Incident: February 11, 2000
Time of Incident: 3:30 p.m.
Location of Incident: Hoopa, California
Significant Causal/Severity Factors:

- Excessive speed
- Failure to negotiate a left curve
- Wheels left the right side of the road
- Overcorrection when attempting to bring right wheels back onto the road surface

Number of Firefighter Fatalities: 1

The Incident:

The 26-year-old male firefighter who was fatally injured was responding as the driver of a 1,000-gallon pumper/tanker en route to a motor vehicle crash on a narrow two-lane road. Another firefighter rode in the right-front seat. Neither firefighter was wearing a seatbelt at the time of the collision.

While the pumper/tanker was about to negotiate a slight left curve, a car approached from the other direction straddling the line between the two lanes. The driver moved the apparatus to the right side of the road to avoid a collision; the pumper/tanker's right tires left the pavement and drove onto a soft grassy shoulder. The truck continued on the shoulder for about 230 feet. In order to avoid a collision with a utility pole, the driver steered sharply to the left. The pumper/tanker began to fishtail, glanced off the power pole on the right side of the road, veered to the left out of control, and struck a large oak tree. The driver was trapped behind the steering wheel, and the passenger was ejected. The driver was extricated after almost an hour of effort.

Although he was alert and conscious during the extrication, the driver entered a coma in the hospital. He never regained consciousness and died on February 14th, which happened to also be his 27th birthday. The passenger who was ejected eventually recovered.

CASE NUMBER 33

Date of Incident: November 2, 2000
Time of Incident: 2:30 a.m.
Location of Incident: Overisel Township, Michigan
Significant Causal/Severity Factors:

- Excessive speed
- Failure to wear seatbelts
- Failure of the fire apparatus to come to a complete stop at an intersection with a stop signal.

Number of Firefighter Fatalities: 1

The Incident:

The 41-year-old female firefighter who was fatally injured in this collision was the passenger in a 2,000-gallon tanker responding to a mutual-aid structure fire involving a turkey farm. Neither the passenger nor the driver was wearing seatbelts at the time of the collision.

As the apparatus approached an intersection, a pickup truck approaching the intersection from the other street was thought by the occupants of the fire apparatus to be yielding the right-of-way to the tanker. The tanker may have slowed before going through the stop sign, but it did not come to a complete stop. As the tanker proceeded through the intersection, it was struck by the pickup at the left rear axle.

The force of the impact deflated the right rear tires of the tanker, and the apparatus began to swerve from side to side. The tanker exited the left side of the roadway, rolled over, and the water tank separated from the chassis. The tanker came to rest upside down, and both firefighters were trapped in the cab.

Firefighters from other departments responding to the fire came upon the accident scene and provided aid. Both firefighters were extricated from the cab. The passenger was pronounced dead at the scene as a result of crushing blunt force chest injuries. Her cause of death was listed as mechanical and positional asphyxiation. The injuries to the tanker driver/operator and the driver of the pickup were not life-threatening.

CASE NUMBER 34

Date of Incident: November 16, 2000
Time of Incident: 8:05 p.m.
Location of Incident: Oakland, Kentucky
Significant Causal/Severity Factors:

- Failure to wear seatbelts
- Fatally injured individual ejected from the apparatus
- Wheels left the right side of the road
- Overcorrection when attempting to bring right wheels back onto the road surface

Number of Firefighter Fatalities: 1

The Incident:

The 19-year-old male firefighter who was fatally injured was the driver of a 1,500-gallon tanker participating in a water shuttle drill. The passenger in the right-front seat was a 17-year-old trainee. Neither the driver nor the trainee was wearing a seatbelt at the time of the collision.

As the tanker traveled down the road, the vehicle's right wheels dropped off the roadway. The driver overcorrected to the left and came back on the road, riding the centerline. He corrected again and went off the roadway on the right-hand side. The tank separated from the vehicle, and the cab came to rest on its top. The driver was partially ejected from the vehicle, and the trainee was fully ejected.

The driver was removed from the vehicle and transported to the hospital by ambulance. He was pronounced dead at the hospital approximately 1 hour after the collision. The trainee was severely injured.

CASE NUMBER 35

Date of Incident: January 12, 2001
Time of Incident: 2:20 p.m.
Location of Incident: Hillsboro, Kentucky
Significant Causal/Severity Factors:
- Excessive speed
- Failure to negotiate a right curve
- Failure to wear seatbelts
- Fatally injured individual ejected from the apparatus
- Wheels left the right side of the road
- Overcorrection when attempting to bring right wheels back onto the road surface

Number of Firefighter Fatalities: 1

The Incident:

The 29-year-old male firefighter was the sole occupant and driver of a tanker responding to a grass fire. The driver, who was the fire chief's son, was not wearing a seatbelt at the time of the collision.

As the tanker came through a right curve, the tanker left the right side of the road. The driver steered it back onto the road surface, crossed the road, and exited the left side of the roadway. The apparatus struck an embankment and a telephone pole and rolled over. The driver was ejected from the vehicle, and the tanker came to rest on top of him.

CASE NUMBER 36

Date of Incident: June 2, 2001
Time of Incident: 4:15 a.m.
Location of Incident: Edgerton, Missouri
Significant Causal/Severity Factors:

- Failure to wear seatbelts
- Fatally injured individual ejected from the apparatus
- Wheels left the right side of the road
- Overcorrection when attempting to bring right wheels back onto the road surface

Number of Firefighter Fatalities: 1

The Incident:

The 30-year-old male firefighter was the right-front seat passenger in a tanker responding to a mutual-aid request for assistance at a structure fire. The firefighter was not wearing a seatbelt at the time of the collision.

As the tanker responded, it met another fire department vehicle responding in the other direction. Although the approaching apparatus stayed in its lane, the driver of the tanker moved to the right to allow the other vehicle to pass. In the process of moving to the right, the right wheels of the tanker left the roadway. The tanker traveled 140 feet on the right shoulder before the driver steered left to bring the truck back on the road. The tanker crossed the road and left the left side of the road and impacted a grassy/rocky hill. The tanker overturned and came to rest 105 feet from the point at which it left the roadway. The firefighter was ejected from the tanker and died at the scene. The driver of the tank was seriously injured but remained in the cab of the tanker during the rollover.

Tragically, a firefighter from a different local fire department was charged with setting the structure fire.

CASE NUMBER 37

Date of Incident: August 19, 2001
Time of Incident: 12:45 p.m.
Location of Incident: Odell, Oregon
Significant Causal/Severity Factors:

- Failure to wear seatbelts
- Mechanical failure (tire blowout)

Number of Firefighter Fatalities: 1

The Incident:

The 52-year-old male driver was returning to his fire district with a 2,000-gallon tanker that had undergone water tank repairs. The driver/operator was the sole occupant of the tanker. The water tank was empty.

While going down the freeway at a speed estimated at 60 miles per hour, the right-front tire of the tanker experienced a blowout. The tanker veered to the right, crossed the shoulder, and went into a level field of grass and rocks. The tanker traveled at an angle through the field for about 300 feet before striking a number of large boulders and a tree.

The cab of the tanker was severely damaged, and the driver/operator was trapped in the vehicle. Responding firefighters removed the driver/operator from the tanker; however, he was pronounced dead at the scene. The cause of death was listed as blunt force trauma to the head, abdomen, and upper and lower extremities.

CASE NUMBER 38

Date of Incident: November 19, 2001
Time of Incident: Not reported, other than daylight hours
Location of Incident: Cameron, West Virginia
Significant Causal/Severity Factors:

- Excessive speed
- Loss of control while descending a grade
- Failure to negotiate a curve

Number of Firefighter Fatalities: 1

The Incident:

The 21-year-old firefighter was the passenger in a 2,000-gallon tanker responding to a mutual-aid brush fire. The driver of the tanker negotiated several turns and changes in grade during the initial response. As the driver attempted to slow down in a turn, the brake pedal went to the floor and no braking effort was accomplished. The driver tried to pump the pedal but was not able to slow the vehicle. The driver told the victim to jump from the vehicle, but he refused and buckled his seatbelt.

The driver drove into a ditch on the side of the road in an attempt to slow the truck while he increased the engine rpms in an attempt to get the truck into gear. The tanker came to the end of the ditch at a sharp turn and jumped back up onto the roadway. The apparatus crossed the roadway and then plunged down a 40- to 50-foot embankment. The truck flipped end over end, and the chassis and the water tank separated. The driver and the victim were trapped in the cab.

An engine company was responding on the same incident and was nearly struck by the water tank as it rolled downhill. After witnessing the crash, the engine company firefighters went to the aid of the trapped firefighters. Both trapped firefighters were talking when the engine company members reached the truck; however, the passenger stopped breathing shortly thereafter. Both firefighters were extricated from the crushed cab. The driver was transported to the hospital by medical helicopter. An autopsy revealed that the passenger died of internal trauma.

The police report cited excessive speed and failure to maintain control as contributing factors in the crash. An inspection of the remains of the tanker found that the rear brakes were out of adjustment.

The following definitions apply to terms as they are used in this report. They may not be industry-wide terms or definitions in all cases.

Antilock Braking System. A computerized braking system that is designed to monitor the spinning of the apparatus wheels and release them when the wheels lock up and begin to force a skid.

Auxiliary Braking Systems. Braking systems, in addition to the service brakes, that are used to assist in slowing the apparatus when the driver removes his or her foot from the throttle pedal.

Baffles. Dividers within a liquid tank that are designed to prevent liquid surges from occurring when the tank is partially full.

Brake Fade. Heating of the brakes that can result in momentary loss of braking ability when the brakes are applied in rapid succession.

Braking Distance. The distance a vehicle travels from the time the brakes are applied until the apparatus comes to a complete stop.

Bridge Gross Weight. A weight rating assigned to a vehicle based on the combination of the vehicle's weight and the distance between its axles.

Call-Back Firefighters. Career or part-paid firefighters who respond from their homes or other locations to the fire station or fire scene when notified of the need to do so.

Candidate. A firefighter who is in training to be come a fire apparatus driver operator.

Career Firefighters. A firefighter who is employed full-time by a fire service organization. The primary occupational mission of the career firefighter is the provision of emergency services to people served by the fire service organization. Career firefighters are most often based in fire stations and deploy from these stations when an emergency occurs.

Causal Factors. Factors that are responsible for the incidence or severity of a collision or accident.

Center of Gravity. The point at which the entire weight of the fire apparatus is considered to be concentrated so that, if supported at this point, the apparatus would remain in equilibrium at any position.

Crash. An event in which an apparatus rolls over or collides with another fixed or moving object.

Driver Reaction Distance. The time period between when a driver recognizes the need to brake and when the braking is actually started.

Driving Course. A grid or circuit of roadways that simulate public thoroughfares. A large, paved driving pad on which various driving exercises may be laid out for the purpose of driver training.

Dump Site. The location in a water shuttle where tankers drop their load of water so that it may be pumped onto the fire or other emergency.

Emergency. An incident in which the potential for death, injury, or property loss are substantial unless expedient actions are taken.

Fill Site. The location in a water shuttle operation where tankers are quickly refilled with water before returning to the emergency scene.

Fire Police. Members, usually of a volunteer fire department, who respond with the fire department and assist the police with traffic control, crowd control, and scene preservation and security; common only in the mid-Atlantic states of the U.S. Also called Special Police.

Fire Pump. A water pump mounted on an apparatus with a rated capacity of at least 250 gallons per minute at 150 psi net pump pressure and used for fire fighting.

Front Gross Axle Weight Rating (FGAWR). The chassis or axle manufacturer's specified maximum load-carrying capability of a vehicle's front axle.

Gross Combination Weight Rating (GCWR). The chassis manufacturer's specified maximum load-carrying capacity of a combination (tractor-trailer) vehicle.

Gross Vehicle Weight Rating (GVWR). The chassis manufacturer's specified maximum load-carrying capability of a vehicle having two axle systems.

Law. A rule of conduct in society that has been adopted by an authority having jurisdiction; there are criminal penalties for failure to abide by such rules.

Liability. The risk of civil damages that may be taken from an individual, organization, or both for failure to act in a reasonable, prudent manner.

Limited-Access Highway. An interstate highway, freeway, turnpike, or other similar thoroughfare in which entrance and exit are only possible from access/egress ramps.

Liquid Surge. The force created by fluid within a tank when the direction or speed of a vehicle carrying the tank changes.

Maintenance. The act of keeping an apparatus in a state of usefulness or readiness.

Mobile Water Supply Apparatus. A vehicle designed primarily for transporting water to fire emergency scenes to be applied by other vehicles or pumping equipment. This term is used primarily by the National Fire Protection Association (NFPA).

Nonemergency. Any condition in which the apparatus is being driven other than when responding to a reported emergency.

Overcorrection. Actions taken by an apparatus driver to correct a problem that in fact lead to a second or larger hazardous situation occurring.

Oversteering. Excessive manipulation of the vehicle's steering system when trying to regain control of an apparatus that is out of control.

Parking Brakes. Brakes that are applied by the driver to prevent the movement of a parked apparatus.

Passenger. A firefighter riding in any position of the apparatus cab other than the driver's position.

Preincident Planning. The process of making plans for an emergency at a given location in advance of an actual emergency.

Pumper-Tanker. Term used to describe a fire department pumper with a water tank of 1,000 gallons or larger. This apparatus may function as either a pumper or a tanker, depending on the needs of the incident.

Reaction Distance. The distance a vehicle travels while a driver is transferring the foot from the accelerator to the brake pedal after perceiving the need for stopping.

Rear Gross Axle Weight Rating (RGAWR). The chassis or axle manufacturer's specified maximum load-carrying capability of a vehicle's rear axle(s).

Repair. To restore or replace that which has become inoperable.

Safety Officer. A fire department official charged with the responsibility for implementing and monitoring the department's overall occupational safety and health program.

Service Brakes. The primary brakes that are manually actuated by the driver via the brake pedal and used to slow or stop a moving apparatus.

Spanner Wrench. A hand-tool used principally to make or break coupling connections and other simple tasks.

Standard. A document of rules or practices that are adopted by an organization that has an interest in a particular topic.

Standard Operating Procedure (SOP). An organization's written plan for carrying out the routine daily functions of that organization.

Surface Streets (Roads). Refers to all those thoroughfares that are not divided or limited-access highways.

Swash Plates. See *Baffles*.

Tanker. See *Mobile Water Supply Apparatus*.

Tender. The Incident Command System (ICS) term for *Tanker*. See *Mobile Water Supply Apparatus*.

Total Stopping Distance. The sum of the driver reaction distance and the vehicle braking distance.

Training Ground. Facility on which firefighter training occurs.

Transfer Pump. A separate engine or PTO-driven water pump mounted on an apparatus with a minimum capacity of 250 gpm at 50 psi net pump pressure and used primarily for water transfer.

Unimproved road surfaces. Used to describe roads that have not been paved with a hard surface such as asphalt or concrete. Unimproved road surfaces include dirt, gravel, sand, stone, and similar material roads.

Volunteer Firefighters. A firefighter who may or may not be compensated for the service he or she provides. Volunteer firefighters provide emergency services to the people served by their organization and generally respond from their home or place of work when an emergency occurs. Depending on department policy, volunteer firefighters may respond to their fire station or directly to the scene of an emergency. Paid-on-call firefighters, since their work is not full-time, are included in this definition.

Water Shuttle. An organized process to move water between a supply source and an emergency scene using fire department tankers.

TRAINING MANUALS AND RELEVANT BOOKS

Emergency Vehicle Driver Training (FA-110); United States Fire Administration, Emmitsburg, MD 21727; www.usfa.fema.gov or 1-800-561-3356

Introduction to Fire Pump Operations by Thomas Sturdevant; Delmar, P.O. Box 15015, Albany, NY 12212; 1-800-998-7498 or www.firescience.com

Pumping Apparatus Driver/Operator Handbook; IFSTA/Fire Protection Publications, 930 North Willis Street, Stillwater, OK 74075; 1-800-654-4055 or www.ifsta.org

The Tire and Rim Year Book; The Tire and Rim Association, Inc., 175 Montrose West Avenue, Suite 150, Copley, OH 44313; 1-330-666-2121 or www.us-tra.org

APPLICABLE NATIONAL FIRE PROTECTION ASSOCIATION STANDARDS

National Fire Protection Association

One Batterymarch Park

Quincy, MA 02269

1-800-344-3555

www.nfpa.org

NFPA 1001, *Standard for Fire Fighter Professional Qualifications*

NFPA 1002, *Standard for Fire Apparatus Driver/Operator Professional Qualifications*

NFPA 1041, *Standard for Fire Service Instructor Professional Qualifications*

NFPA 1071, *Standard for Emergency Vehicle Technician Professional Qualifications*

NFPA 1142, *Standard on Water Supplies for Suburban and Rural Fire Fighting*

NFPA 1451, *Standard for a Fire Service Vehicle Operations Training Program*

NFPA 1500, *Standard on Fire Department Occupational Health and Safety Program*

NFPA 1901, *Standard for Automotive Fire Apparatus*

NFPA 1911, *Standard for Service Tests of Fire Pump Systems on Fire Apparatus*

NFPA 1915, *Standard for Fire Apparatus Preventive Maintenance Program*

NFPA 1932, *Standard on Use, Maintenance, and Service Testing of Fire Department Ground Ladders*

Training Programs

Emergency Vehicle Operations Course; Volunteer Firemen's Insurance Services, P.O. Box 2726, York, PA 17405; 1-800-233-1957 or www.vfis.com

National Association for Professional Driving, 1001A South Interstate 45, P.O. Box 649, Hutchins, Texas 75141-0649; (214) 225-7366 or www.napd.com

Pumping Apparatus Driver/Operator Handbook Curriculum Package; IFSTA/Fire Protection Publications, 930 North Willis Street, Stillwater, OK 74075; 1-800-654-4055 or www.ifsta.org

San Bernadino County Sheriff's Emergency Vehicle Operations Center, 18958 Institution Road, San Bernadino, CA 92407; 1-909-887-7550 or www.evoc.org

Videotapes

Aerial Apparatus Driving Techniques; produced by Action Training Systems, available through IFSTA/Fire Protection Publications, 930 North Willis Street, Stillwater, OK 74075; 1-800-654-4055 or www.ifsta.org

Emergency Vehicle Driving series (13 tapes); Fire and Emergency Television Network; 1-800-932-3386 or www.fetn.com

Safe Operation of Emergency Vehicles; produced by Action Training Systems, available through IFSTA/Fire Protection Publications, 930 North Willis Street, Stillwater, OK 74075; 1-800-654-4055 or www.ifsta.org

Websites

Dr. Driving's Page for Driving Emergency Vehicles; www.aloha.net/dyc/emergency.html

Other Sources of Information Used for this Report

America's Experience with Seat Belt and Child Seat Use; National Highway Transportation Safety Administration, Washington, DC; August, 2001; www.nhtsa.dot.gov

Apparatus Accidents: Causes and Circumstances; Solomon, Stephen S.; *Fire Engineering Magazine*, May, 1983

Apparatus Color Update; Solomon, Stephen S.; *Fire Chief Magazine*, February, 1982

Bridge Gross Weight Formula; United States Department of Transportation (HTO-33/revised 4-84), Office of Traffic Operations

The Case For Lime-Yellow: Can It Reduce Serious Apparatus Accidents?; Solomon, Stephen S.; *Firehouse*, May, 1991

Firefighter Fatalities in the United States in 1999; United States Fire Administration, Emmitsburg, MD, June, 2000; www.fema.gov/usfa

Manual on Uniform Traffic Control Devices; Federal Highway Administration; 2001 Edition; www.fhwa.dot.gov

Press Release: U.S. Transportation Secretary Mineta Announces Results of Seat Belt Study (NHSTA 10-01); National Highway Transportation Safety Administration, Washington, DC; www.nhtsa.dot.gov

Traffic Safety Facts 1999: Large Trucks (DOT HS 809 088); National Highway Transportation Safety Administration, Washington, DC; www.nhtsa.dot.gov

Traffic Safety Facts 1999: Occupant Protection (DOT HS 809 090); National Highway Transportation Safety Administration, Washington, DC; www.nhtsa.dot.gov

Wear Your Seat Belt; Capital District Commuter Register, Washington, DC; August 5, 2001; www.commuter-register.org

What Color Is Best?; Solomon, Stephen S.; *Fire Chief Magazine*, 1971

SAMPLE APPARATUS MAINTENANCE AND INSPECTION FORMS

Weekly Emergency Vehicle Report

Page No. _____

Name of Company _____

Address _____

Emergency Vehicle MFG. _____

Year _____ Serial No. _____ Type _____

Required Tire Pressure: _____

Date Inspection Completed	Inspector	Battery Check	Braking System	Electrical System, Lights & Sirens	Tires & Wheel Lugs	Fuel Level	Oil Level Eng & Hyd	Hydraulic System	Pump Check	Cooling System	Lubrication Pump & Ladder	Engine Check	Booster Tank Level	Doors - Compartment & Cab	Portable Equipment	Special Remarks On Road Test Inspection Use Other Side

REMARKS: (Please itemize procedure taken on unsatisfactory inspection items noted on opposite side)

Inspection Date:	Repair Date:	Comments:	Repairs Completed - By:	Date:

Printed in U.S.A.

Item No. C10:007

Emergency Vehicle
Maintenance Record Card

Vehicle
Description

Model Year

Manufacturer's
Serial No.

Plate No.

Tire Record

Make	Warranty (Life)	Date Installed	Odometer

Battery Record

Motor Oil & Oil Filter Record

Date	Months Or Miles	Quarts Of Oil	Filter	Remarks

Lubrication Record

Date	Remarks	Date	Remarks

C10:005

Printed in U.S.A.

Maintenance And Repair Record

Date	Nature Of Repairs & / Or Maintenance Service	Repaired By	Cost

Emergency Vehicle
Driver's Safety Check

Date   Odometer Reading   Unit No.

Pre-Trip Inspection   Post-Trip Inspection

Only Items Checked Require Attention

Gauges - Ammeter, Oil Pressure, Fuel,
Water Temperature, Air Pressure or
Vacuum
Windshield Wipers
Windshield & Windows
Heater & Defroster
Mirrors
Brakes (Foot & Parking)
Engine Noises
Horn & Sirens
Steering
Vehicle Body
Wheels, Tires, Lugs
Fuel Tank & Cap
Leaks - Water, Fuel, Oil

Head Lights
Tail Lights
Stop Lights
Turn Signals & 4-Way Flasher
Reflectors
Emergency Equipment
     Other - If Applicable
Clearance Lights
Emergency Warning Lights
Side Marker Lights
Brake Hoses
Compartment Door Locks
Drain Air Tanks of Moisture
Air Systems
Mounted Equipment

Remarks (explain unsatisfactory items noted above)

Signature of Driver

To Be Completed by Repair Shop

Mechanic's Report (If defects are noted)

Signature of Repair Shop
Foreman or Mechanic

Date

(Use back of form for additional remarks.)

Item No. C10:006

Emergency Vehicle
Driver's Safety Check

Date   Odometer Reading   Unit No.

Pre-Trip Inspection   Post-Trip Inspection

Only Items Checked Require Attention

Gauges - Ammeter, Oil Pressure, Fuel,
Water Temperature, Air Pressure or
Vacuum
Windshield Wipers
Windshield & Windows
Heater & Defroster
Mirrors
Brakes (Foot & Parking)
Engine Noises
Horn & Sirens
Steering
Vehicle Body
Wheels, Tires, Lugs
Fuel Tank & Cap
Leaks - Water, Fuel, Oil

Head Lights
Tail Lights
Stop Lights
Turn Signals & 4-Way Flasher
Reflectors
Emergency Equipment
     Other - If Applicable
Clearance Lights
Emergency Warning Lights
Side Marker Lights
Brake Hoses
Compartment Door Locks
Drain Air Tanks of Moisture
Air Systems
Mounted Equipment

Remarks (explain unsatisfactory items noted above)

Signature of Driver

To Be Completed by Repair Shop

Mechanic's Report (If defects are noted)

Signature of Repair Shop
Foreman or Mechanic

Date

(Use back of form for additional remarks.)

Item No. C10:006

ADDITIONAL INFORMATION ON FIRE APPARATUS ANTILOCK AND AUXILIARY BRAKING SYSTEMS AND OPERATION

The following articles were written by Michael Wilbur of Emergency Vehicle Response, Inc. and the Fire Department of the City of New York (FDNY) and originally appeared in *Firehouse* magazine. They are reprinted here with the magazine and author's permission.

EMERGENCY BRAKING: CAN I REALLY STOP THIS FIRE TRUCK?
(SEPTEMBER, 1997 ISSUE)

In my July 1997 column, I compiled a top 10 list for emergency vehicle operators. One item on the list involved emergency braking. This column will expand your knowledge of emergency braking procedures.

Emergency braking is probably the least known and the most misunderstood operation that we perform behind the wheel of an emergency vehicle. Yet it is probably the most important factor in accident avoidance. But why?

When I teach an emergency vehicle operators' class, I will ask the question: "How many apparatus operators in this class have ever had to make a life-or-death emergency stop in the fire apparatus?" Inevitably, two or three operators will raise their hands, in a class of 30 operators. That means only about 10% or less of the operators that I have surveyed have ever had to make an emergency stop.

You will have a better understanding of this phenomenon if we examine events closely and in chronological order. We start at the fire station and find the apparatus backed into the bay, positioned similarly to a NASA rocket, ready to blast off. Then we add the next component, the apparatus operator – in this case a nervous operator; the next alarm will be his first as an emergency vehicle operator.

The alarm sounds. He feels a rush of adrenaline as he mounts the apparatus and begins to respond. He is tentative, even nervous, as he responds at a respectable 20-30 mph. Time passes, he drives to a few more alarms, his confidence builds, his speed increases to 30-40 mph.

Then, his attitude changes. This apparatus driving is easy; people get out of his way when he turns on his lights and sirens (theoretically), the fire apparatus handles like a car, speed increases to 40-50 mph. A few months, then a few years go by.

As time passes, his confidence increases proportionally with speed and safety decreases, as complacency sets in. Now the driver has 10-15 years' driving experience, everyone gets out of his way and there is no situation that his driving abilities cannot handle. EXCEPT – he has never had to make a sudden serious emergency stop.

Think about it. How many emergency stops have you had to make in your driving career? Have there been any? If you've never had to make a sudden stop, it now becomes much easier to respond at 50-60 mph. Maybe if apparatus operators had the awesome experience of bringing a 40,000-, 50,000- or 60,000-pound fire apparatus to an emergency stop at 50 mph maybe they would not do 50 mph any more. It becomes really easy in a modern fire apparatus to go really fast if you have never really had to stop.

How do you train operators on emergency braking procedures? First, you must identify the correct braking procedure. Three braking procedures come to mind.

The first emergency braking procedure is brake lockup. This occurs when the vehicle operator panics, holds the brake pedal to the floor in a vehicle not equipped with antilock brakes. When lockup occurs, the driver loses all operational and steering control. Why? It's a matter of physics. The driver's ability to keep the vehicle under control is a direct result of friction between the vehicle's tires and the road surface.

When the brakes lock up, most of the friction is lost, causing the apparatus to skid out of control. If you are trying to steer when the brakes are locked, you will continue to straighten even if the wheels are turned to the left or right. Also with the brakes locked up, the friction is drastically reduced and it takes a much greater distance to stop. This braking procedure is obviously not the answer.

Next, we investigate the stab braking procedure. Stab braking occurs when the operator continually activates the brake with quick brake depressions or by pumping the brakes. With stab braking, there are multiple brake applications in a short period of time, thereby depleting the air supply for the brakes. This in turn could prematurely activate the maxi-brakes on the apparatus which could cause the brakes to lock up. Remember, under U.S. Department of Transportation (DOT) standards maxi-brakes on the apparatus will begin to activate at 60 psi. Although stab braking is better than locking up the brakes, the most efficient, safe, braking procedure is threshold braking.

Threshold braking is accomplished when the operator depresses the brake pedal until just prior to wheel lockup. Then, the operator is supposed to ease up on the brake pedal, keeping the tires rotating, which causes friction. When the operator is assured the wheels are moving, he or she again depresses the brake and keeps repeating the procedure until the vehicle comes to a complete stop.

This is a great procedure in theory; the reality is that the driver will probably panic, lock the wheels and lose control of the apparatus. The threshold braking procedure is the manual equivalent of antilock brakes. Although antilock brakes will be covered in a future column, there are several things you need to know about antilock brakes.

Antilock brakes are now required on most fire apparatus as per National Fire Protection Association (NFPA) 1901, the motorized fire apparatus standard (August 1996).

Antilock brakes must be applied with steady, even pressure on the brake pedal and not the threshold braking procedure. It is imperative that the operator identify antilock brake equipped apparatus, prior to the movement of the apparatus.

I recently taught an emergency vehicle operators' course for a department that had a rescue truck that was 6 months old. Very few drivers knew that the rescue truck was equipped with antilock brakes and nobody understood how antilock brakes work. This was an accident waiting to happen.

Unfortunately, this situation is not unique to that fire department. I have said it before and I will say it again: in many cases we simply just do not know enough about what we are trying to do. With the introduction of electronics, technology and special systems, fire apparatus have become more complex and the fire service has fallen behind in understanding these complexities. What are the answers? Emergency braking training sessions and a driver's manual.

What preparation is necessary for emergency braking exercises? First and foremost, all apparatus must have successfully completed a DOT heavy-duty truck inspection and must be in top mechanical shape.

Next, find an appropriate location in which to conduct the test. We found a school with long, flat entrance and exit roads. We received permission to use the school facilities on a Sunday. We also arranged to have the emergency braking drill videotaped from two different angles.

We assigned a driver and one firefighter to be seated and belted in the cab. The first apparatus was sent down the entrance road attaining a speed of 50 mph. Upon passing the first set of traffic cones, the driver began to threshold brake. Drivers were given prior instruction that locking the brakes up was unacceptable and an unsafe act. Prior to the test, information had been compiled on the apparatus, including engine size, horsepower, transmission type, pumping size, booster tank size and auxiliary braking devices, if the apparatus was so equipped. Other information included vehicle height, overall length, width, weight, and wheelbase.

All the information and the distances needed to stop each of the apparatus were recorded. These measurements represent the total stopping distance for each of the apparatus included in the testing. Two emergency braking tests were completed on each of the seven apparatus that took part in the exercise. The average stopping distance was 154.83 feet, at an average speed 48.91 mph, during the 14 emergency braking tests that were done.

The drivers who took part in the exercise now realize the limitation put on them by apparatus, their environment and even themselves. These limitations include, but are not limited to, the size of the vehicle, vehicle weight, speed, water surge, condition of the brakes and tires, road conditions, and the driver's ability and experience. Drivers also learned that these limitations are all interconnected and that they drastically affect the driver's ability to stop in an emergency.

What about the videotape of the emergency braking test? The tapes can be used for indoor driver training. Also, the tape could be invaluable in any future litigation. Although the test results are valid only for that date and time, they will prove to an outside third party that the department has some degree of competence and knowledge in the operation of its emergency vehicles.

I have another idea that may be helpful to apparatus manufacturers and apparatus operators. The apparatus manufacturer should provide a driver's manual. Unlike the owner's manual that is long, technical, and confusing and usually locked in the chief's office, the driver's manual would be made available to all persons involved in the light maintenance and the operation of each vehicle. The driver's manual would be well organized, easy to understand, and easy to read.

Why would the apparatus manufacturers look positively on this idea? It could save them hundreds or thousands of dollars on warranty work that could be avoided if the drivers had a better understanding of what they were trying to do. It would make the operation of emergency vehicles safer, which would benefit everyone. Anyone from the NFPA 1901 committee interested?

BRAKING PROCEDURES
(NOVEMBER, 1997 ISSUE)

This month, we continue with the second part of a series of columns on braking procedures for emergency vehicle operators. Part 1 looked at emergency braking procedures (September 1997). Now, we will examine in chronological order those events that must occur to bring a fire apparatus to a safe stop. To do this we must first define the terms used in braking.

The first point that must be made is that a fire apparatus will travel a great distance from the point where the operator first realizes the need to stop and where the fire apparatus actually comes to a complete stop. The first part of that distance traveled is referred to as the "perception distance" – the distance your apparatus travels from the time you spot a problem until you decide what corrective action to take. Another way to describe this is as the distance the apparatus will travel from the time your eyes spot a problem until your brain receives this signal, processes the information, and then makes a decision on what action or actions to take.

The next part of that distance traveled is referred to as "reaction distance," or the distance your apparatus will travel while you move your foot from the accelerator to the brake pedal. This distance can be substantially reduced if the operator puts his or her foot over the brake at the first sign of a potential problem. This is also called "covering the brake."

If the operator covers the brake, the vehicle can save 1.1 feet for every mile per hour of speed. For example, if the fire apparatus is traveling at 50 mph and the driver covers the brake as danger is perceived ahead, the fire apparatus will save 55 feet (50 mph x 1.1 feet = 55 feet). The distance saved by covering the brake could be the difference between having and not having an accident. If your apparatus is equipped with auxiliary braking devices, you will stop even sooner, as many of these devices are activated when you lift your foot off the accelerator. The time it takes for the operator to move his or her foot to the brake from the accelerator is the driver's reaction time. The average driver's reaction time is three-quarters of a second. However, if the driver is drunk, on drugs, fatigued, or has aged to the point that hearing, eyesight or reflexes are affected; the reaction time is going to be substantially longer. Accident investigation experts have said that at night the average driver's reaction time could be as much as 1½ seconds.

The next distance traveled is "brake lag distance"; that is the distance the apparatus travels after you apply the brakes and before they actuate. Brake lag distance is applicable only for vehicles equipped with air brakes. If you have a vehicle equipped with hydraulic-type brakes, there is no brake lag because depressing the brake pedal compresses a liquid that has an instantaneous reaction on the brakes. Air brakes are extremely reliable and completely safe. However, when the brake pedal is depressed in a vehicle equipped with air brakes, there is a momentary delay. This delay occurs when the brake pedal is depressed. It then triggers a release of air from the air-holding tanks, which in turn travels through the brake lines and actuates the brakes.

The last distance we travel is the "braking distance" – the distance your apparatus travels after the brakes take hold until the apparatus comes to a complete stop.

By adding all the distances together you have the "total stopping distance." The equation looks like this:

PERCEPTION DISTANCE + REACTION DISTANCE + BRAKE LAG DISTANCE

+ BRAKING DISTANCE = TOTAL STOPPING DISTANCE

Although this is the standard formula for computing stopping distances, many other factors can affect how long it will take to bring your fire apparatus to a complete and safe stop:

Brake fade. When there are multiple brake applications in a short period of time, particularly when the vehicle involved is carrying a lot of weight going down a steep grade, the brakes overheat. As the brakes overheat, they are said to be glazed over, which reduces friction; this in turn will cause the brakes to fail.

Speed. The faster the apparatus is moving, the longer it takes to stop the apparatus.

Weight. Too much weight could cause the weight to overrun the brakes (brake fade) and could cause brake failure. Not enough weight; driving a tractor-trailer combination without the trailer (bobtailing). Many tractor-trailer drivers who have had to bobtail a tractor will be able to tell you about harrowing experiences, this writer included.

The forward surge of the water in your tanks. With water weighing eight-plus pounds per gallon and with most tank sizes ranging from 1,000 to 4,000 gallons, one would only have to do the calculations to realize that we are trying to stop 8,000 to 32,000 pounds of water weight in motion. This water weight in motion is not only front to back but also side to side.

Hills. It takes longer to stop going down a hill than it does to stop going uphill or on level pavement. Forward momentum and gravity.

Wet or slippery surfaces. Driving in any kind of inclement weather will affect your ability to stop. One good example comes to mind for this time of year is driving on wet leaves. It's like driving on ice.

Type of road surface. It takes a greater distance to stop on gravel, dirt or a sandy surface than it does to stop on concrete or blacktop. I recall in accident investigation and reconstruction classes at which much time was spent describing the coefficient of friction for each surface and how it affects a vehicle's ability to stop.

Condition of brakes and tires. New brakes and new tires mean less distance it takes to stop. Worn brakes and worn tires mean more distance it takes to stop.

The driver. A driver who is drunk, on drugs, fatigued, lacks good reflexes, has a poor attitude, or has a lack of experience will affect the stopping distances.

There are some braking tips that can be offered here: slower is safer. You must control the apparatus, don't let the apparatus control you. All apparatus must be kept in top shape. Train your drivers so that they may handle specific traffic situations, such as hills, different road surfaces, slippery road surfaces, or any other situations specific to your jurisdiction.

AUXILIARY BRAKING SYSTEMS
(JANUARY, 1998 ISSUE)

The two previous columns investigated emergency braking (September 1997) and braking procedures (November 1997). The braking series has now grown from three parts to four parts. This month, we will learn about auxiliary braking systems and in the next column we will discuss traction control systems.

Auxiliary braking systems are not anything new, having first been developed in Europe in the early 1930s. However, these systems did not gain wide acceptance in the U.S. until the 1970s and '80s. Now, auxiliary braking systems are the general rule rather than the exception on modern heavy trucks.

Fire apparatus are no exception as it relates to auxiliary braking systems. In the current National Fire Protection Association (NFPA) 1901 fire apparatus standard, all apparatus with a gross vehicle weight rating (GVWR) of 36,000 pounds or greater shall be equipped with an auxiliary braking system. The standard also states that the purchaser of apparatus with a GVWR of 31,000 pounds or greater should consider equipping it with an auxiliary braking system.

Fire apparatus commonly make repeated stops from high speeds, which cause rapid brake lining wear and a brake fade, sometimes leading to accidents.

Auxiliary braking systems are recommended on apparatus that are exposed regularly to steep or long grades, are operating in congested areas where repeated stops are normal or respond to a high number of emergencies.

Some auxiliary braking devices should be disconnected when the apparatus is operated on slippery surfaces. Follow the auxiliary braking device manufacturers' recommendations for proper instructions. Section 35002 (2) of the California Vehicle Code states, "Any fire apparatus exceeding 31,000 pounds gross vehicle weight rating (GVWR) shall be equipped with a retarder". Also of interest – California requires special driving licenses for fire apparatus operators. It would appear California is years ahead of most states in fire apparatus driving safety.

Why are retarders mandated today, when they were not even considered 40 years ago when the technology first became available in the U.S.? What has changed in apparatus design to require the use of auxiliary braking devices? If you have followed the evolution of fire apparatus, the answer becomes quite apparent: the increase in engine horsepower.

Engine horsepower has more than doubled in the last 30 years, from less than 250 hp to modern-day electronic diesels that can develop more than 500 hp. This increase in horsepower has raised average speed dramatically. When I drove our 1947 Mack pumper it could not go over 50 mph; now, our 1992 pumper would have no trouble going over 70 mph.

Gross vehicle weight also plays an important role in the need for auxiliary braking systems. Prior to 1960, a typical pumper had a 300- to 500-gallon booster tank, three or four compartments, and carried three firefighters safely. Pumpers from this era had GVWR of 20,000 to 30,000 pounds. Present-day pumpers have 750- to 1,500-gallon booster tanks; 10 compartments or more are not uncommon; and enclosed cabs capable of carrying 5 to 10 firefighters are now the norm. Today, pumpers have GVWR of 30,000-50,000 pounds and many ladder trucks, tankers, and heavy rescue apparatus exceed 70,000 pounds GVWR.

With better drive trains, tires and aerodynamics, there is less wind resistance or other passive resistance that would hold the apparatus back or act as a natural brake. There have been great developmental strides made in standard service brakes but their capacities are limited. The performance achieved in endurance braking has improved dramatically over the recent past, due to significant increases in engine power, vehicle speeds and payload, coupled with reduced engine retarding, rolling resistance and aero-dynamic drag. Service brakes, however, have not been able to match the increase in demand upon them as a result of several limitations.

One limitation on service brakes is the size of the wheels, which are becoming smaller; this in turn creates less surface area for braking. Another limitation is the width of the brakes which are restricted due to the spring; and suspension components, again reducing surface area. Auxiliary braking devices have been designed to provide safe, long-duration braking that conventional brakes, in spite of their superior performances in emergency or stopping situations, cannot provide. For these reasons, it is necessary that auxiliary braking systems provide the greater part of the braking effort, thus leaving the service brakes free to operate under full efficiency when required for emergency stopping.

There are four types of auxiliary braking systems:

- Exhaust brakes
- Engine brakes
- Hydraulic retarders
- Electric retarders

The exhaust brake, also known as a compression brake, is an auxiliary braking device used to help slow a vehicle's forward momentum. This slowing power is achieved by restricting the flow of exhaust gases and increasing back pressure inside the engine (you may have done this by putting an apple, snowball, or other obstruction in an exhaust pipe). This increased back pressure creates resistance against the pistons in the engine, slowing the crankshaft's rotation, and ultimately helping to slow the vehicle's forward momentum.

The exhaust brake is usually activated by a dashboard switch. The switch needs to be in the off position before the vehicle can be started. With the dashboard switch in the on position, the vehicle operator need only lift his or her foot off the accelerator and/or clutch, if the vehicle is so equipped, to make the system operate. Engine speed has a major effect on exhaust brake performance.

As with all auxiliary braking systems, the exhaust brake is not intended to stop the vehicle but to aid in controlling speed. On an uphill climb with the exhaust brake on, taking your foot off the accelerator will result in rapid vehicle slowdown because of the uphill grade and the retarding power of the exhaust brake. Manufacturers recommend never using the exhaust brake on wet or icy road surfaces and only using the exhaust brake only when you have good, dry traction with the road's surface.

Before shutting off your engine, always turn your exhaust brake off or you may not be able to restart the engine. It is also recommended that if you are going to leave your vehicle idling for more than three minutes, the exhaust brake must be shut off. The exhaust brake must also be shut off prior to engaging the pump. It would appear the exhaust brake is better suited for over-the-road trucking rather than the stop-and-go driving of fire apparatus.

The engine brake is a diesel engine auxiliary braking system that uses the engine itself to aid in slowing and controlling the vehicle. When activated, the engine brake alters the operation of the engine's exhaust valves so that the engine works as a power absorbing air compressor. This provides a retarding action to the wheels. The operation of the engine brake is fully automatic once it is turned on.

Depending on the type of engine, the controls for the engine brake consist of one or two switches mounted on the dashboard. The one-switch system usually has three positions – off, low, and high. The off position is self-explanatory.

The low position will give you auxiliary braking in half the engine's cylinders. If you have a six-cylinder diesel, you will receive auxiliary braking in three of the six cylinders. When the switch is in the high position, you will receive auxiliary braking from all six cylinders. This system is often referred to as the two-speed system.

The three-speed system, used on in-line diesel engines, is controlled by two switches. The master switch turns the engine brake on and off; the second switch, which performs the progressive braking function, controls the amount of retarding. The number 1, or low, position gives the operator auxiliary braking from two cylinders; the number 2, or medium, position provides auxiliary braking from four cylinders; and the number 3, or high, position provides auxiliary braking from all six cylinders. If the engine brake does not have the progressive braking feature, your vehicle will be equipped with one switch, with on and off positions that control all of the engine's cylinders.

There are many safety concerns that you must be aware of before using the engine brake. Be sure that the vehicle is maintaining traction and stability using the natural retarding of the engine alone. Because the operation of any vehicle under slippery conditions is unpredictable, be sure you have plenty of distance when testing service brakes of your engine brake.

If you have never driven a vehicle equipped with an engine brake, it is recommended that you do not use it on slick roads until you have some experience with it on dry pavement. When you have that experience, you can use the following operating sequence as a guideline for inclement weather. Make sure the apparatus is maintaining traction before activating the engine brake. If the apparatus is maintaining traction, the engine brake switch can be turned to the low setting. If the apparatus continues to maintain traction, and there is no tendency for the drive wheels to lose traction, you can move the switch to the high position. If the drive wheels tend to lock, immediately switch the engine brake into the low position. Do not attempt to use the high setting until road conditions improve. Never skip steps, i.e.: going from off to high in inclement weather or chances are you will lose control and get into an accident. If you have only an on/off switch and the vehicle fails to maintain traction, turn the engine brake off.

Now that safety concerns have been addressed, you can turn the engine brake on and begin to operate the apparatus. If the vehicle is equipped with an automatic transmission, the engine brake is activated when you move your foot off the throttle, and is deactivated when you reapply pressure to the throttle. There is a pressure-sensing switch that deactivates the engine brake when the apparatus slows to about 10 mph to prevent stalling the engine. However, with the new electronic transmissions this may not be the case. Check your owner's manual to be sure. Also, an engine brake with a pressure-sensing switch must be turned off prior to engaging the pump or you risk stalling the engine. Remember, the apparatus is only being slowed by the engine brake to 10 mph; you must apply the service brakes to come to a complete stop.

The hydraulic retarder is located in or around the automatic transmission housing. It is important to note that the hydraulic retarder is also referred to as a transmission retarder. Hydraulic retarder braking is accomplished when transmission oil is directed into the retarder housing. The oil causes a resistance to rotation of the vaned rotor that is then transferred to the rotor shaft. The retardation power is transmitted through the transmission to the drive train and then to the drive wheels, slowing the vehicle.

Partial braking can be done by moving the manual control valve part way to regulate the oil pressure to the retarder. This manual control valve is located in or around the dash by the steering wheel. With the manual control valve in the off position, oil is removed from the retarder, leaving no drag on the rotor and no auxiliary braking. The heat generated by the absorption of the horsepower within the transmission is dissipated by the transmission oil being circulated through a transmission oil cooler.

There are two types of hydraulic retarders: output and input. It would appear that the output retarder is better suited for fire apparatus use, because of our lower speeds and the stop-and-go traffic that we must contend with. There are several ways to activate a hydraulic retarder: manually by a dashboard switch; letting off on the throttle; applying the service brakes; or a combination of these. Engine exhaust brakes cannot be operated simultaneously with a hydraulic retarder, as that could damage the transmission.

As with the other auxiliary braking systems, caution must be exercised with hydraulic retarders. Manufacturers recommend not using hydraulic retarders in inclement weather or when road surfaces are slippery. The retarder must be turned off by the dashboard switch. However, if the apparatus is equipped with an anti-lock braking system (ABS), it should be equipped with a sensor that interacts with the hydraulic retarder. This sensor will detect wheel lockup and automatically cut back or turn off the retarding force before wheel lockup occurs. If the apparatus is equipped with this ABS interface, it should not have a dashboard on/off switch.

The electric retarder, also known as a driveline retarder, can be mounted on the driveshaft, the transmission, or the rear axle. Three main systems make up the electric retarder: the operator controls, the electronic controller and the rotor/stator assembly. The operator controls consist of using a dashboard switch, letting up on the throttle, depressing the service brakes, or a combination of these.

On apparatus without ABS, but ones that have foot controls, there is also a system on/off switch. The electronic controller is a device that connects the electric retarder to the operator controls and the electrical system of the vehicle. The controller incorporates an electronic speed switch and the ABS interface. To prevent unnecessary discharging of the vehicle's batteries, the electronic switch automatically shuts off the driveline brake when the vehicle has come to a complete stop. The ABS interface deactivates the electric retarder when the ABS system detects imminent wheel lockup.

How does the electric retarder work? By relying on a force as old as gravity, electromagnetism. A stator carrying electromagnets is attached the vehicle chassis or a vehicle drive train component. Two discs are connected to the vehicle drive shaft, resting on each side of the stator, separated from the stator only by a narrow air gap. When the operator activates the driveline brake, coils are energized and produce magnetic fields with alternate polarities. Magnetic flux flows through the coils and rotating discs, creating electromagnetic eddy currents. These currents create a drag on the rotors, without the use of friction. The braking energy is converted into heat that is dissipated through the self-air-cooled discs. A light bar is mounted on the dashboard to indicate the level of retarding power selected. There are generally four lights; each one represents 25% of the available retarding force being used.

There are many advantages to equipping emergency apparatus with an auxiliary braking system: having two braking systems increases safety increases the life of the service brakes, decreases brake maintenance and associated costs, and is effective for city or highway driving.

This column was written to give you an overview of the auxiliary braking systems available today and to provide fire apparatus operators with basic knowledge of the operation of an auxiliary braking system. If your apparatus is equipped with an auxiliary braking system, you need to consult the owner's manual for specific operational guidelines. I would like to thank all of the auxiliary brake manufacturers that provided information for this column.

ANTILOCK BRAKES, TRACTION CONTROL, OTHER GIZMOS, & GADGETS
(March, 1998 Issue)

In our continuing series on emergency vehicle brakes, this month we will look at the dashboard switches that control braking, traction, and other special systems.

The apparatus operator's position could rival the cockpit of a jumbo jet, with all of the switches, gizmos, and gadgets inherent in today's fire vehicles. Technology has increased apparatus safety, yet many people in the fire service have become overwhelmed, including apparatus assemblers, mechanics, driver trainers, and the drivers themselves. Driver trainers with whom I have spoken are struggling to have drivers meet minimum driving standards without introducing specialized topics such as these. Moreover, where would driver trainers look for the information? Unless you have hours to look through the owners' manuals – and if you could find or understand them – very little has been written on the subject. I hope this column fills that void.

There are two switches that are commonly found on apparatus dashboards that we should discuss. One switch controls the operation of the front brake-limiting valves (the slippery-road/dry-road switch). Its original intent was to help the driver maintain control of the apparatus on wet or slippery surfaces. This was accomplished by reducing the air pressure by 50% on the front steering axle when the limiting valve was placed in the slippery-road position. This in turn would prevent the front steering axle from locking up, letting the apparatus operator steer the vehicle even if the rear wheels were locked up and skidding.

That sounds good in principle but in fact it doesn't work. The apparatus loses 25% of its braking capabilities – and that's a vehicle with new or well-maintained brakes. If the brakes are worn or out of adjustment and you have only 60% of the vehicle's original braking capability, by activating the slippery-road switch you diminish the vehicle's ability to stop by an additional 25%. The odds are not in your favor for completing a safe response.

Furthermore, the National Transportation Safety Board (NTSB), after investigating many apparatus accidents, concluded that using manual brake-limiting valves can diminish a rig's stopping capability and, therefore, use of the valves should be discontinued. To be safe, put the switch in the dry position and disconnect it so that accidental activation does not occur. Front brake-limiting valves were standard equipment before the adoption in 1975 of Federal Motor Vehicle Safety Standard 121. That does not mean, however, that the limiting valves were discontinued after 1975; I have seen them on apparatus constructed as late as 1984.

The second switch controls the inter-axle differential lock on the rear tandem axles of the tanker. The inter-axle differential is also known as a "power divider" or "third" differential.

The inter-axle differential is a driver-controlled switch, usually air activated, for a traction device that allows for speed difference between the forward and rear tandem axles while providing equal pulling power from each axle of the tandem. By activating the switch, improved traction is provided for each axle.

How does the system work? The inter-axle differential divides the power equally between the two axles of a tandem. It does not allow the total torque of both axles to exceed twice the torque of the least amount of traction. The inter-axle differential lock mechanically deactivates the inter-axle differential providing maximum traction potential from both axles of a tandem.

Under normal operating conditions, the inter-axle differential switch should be in the unlocked position. Lock the inter-axle differential when approaching or anticipating poor driving conditions to provide improved traction. Always unlock the inter-axle differential when the road conditions improve. When engaging the inter-axle differential lock, you must provide an interruption in torque to the drive train (lift your foot from the accelerator).

Activating the inter-axle differential switch is similar to shifting a manual transmission with a clutch. Do not actuate the inter-axle differential switch while one or more wheels are actually slipping, spinning, or losing traction, or damage to the axle can result. Do not spin the wheels with the inter-axle differential unlocked, or damage to the axle could result.

Unmatched tires on tandem drive axles will cause tire wear and scuffing as well as possible damage to the drive units. The four largest tires should never be installed on one driving axle or the four smallest tires on the other axle.

Such tire mounting will cause an inter-axle "fight" and could damage the drive units. Consequently, experts recommend tires be matched to within ⅛-inch of the same rolling radius and ⅛-inch of the same rolling circumference. This procedure should not be tried on the first response after reading this; however, it's an excellent subject to cover in an inclement-weather driving drill.

Automatic traction control (ATC) is an option available on vehicles equipped with antilock braking systems (ABS). It helps improve traction when vehicles are on slippery surfaces by reducing drive wheel overspin.

The ATC works automatically in two ways. The first way occurs when a drive wheel starts to spin; the ATC applies air pressure to brake the wheel. This transfers engine torque to the wheels with better traction. The second way occurs when all the drive wheels spin. In this case, the ATC reduces engine torque to provide improved traction. The ATC turns itself on and off; drivers do not have to select this feature. If drive wheels spin during acceleration, the ATC green indicator light comes on, indicating the ATC is engaged and working. Also, the engine speed will be decreased as needed until traction is acquired to move the chassis.

A snow-and-mud switch option is included with the ATC. This function increases available traction on extra-soft surfaces like snow, mud, or gravel by slightly increasing the permissible wheel spin. When the apparatus operator activates the snow-and-mud switch, the ATC light blinks continuously. To deactivate the snow-and-mud switch, the operator can press the switch again or turn off the ignition. When this feature is deactivated, the ATC light stops blinking. The snow-and-mud switch must be turned off once the vehicle regains normal traction.

If it is desired to rock the apparatus and the ATC has cut the throttle back, depress the mud-and-snow switch. Caution must be used when depressing the mud-and-snow switch; if the wheel suddenly regains traction, axle damage can occur. The green ATC light will go out when the drive wheels stop spinning. (Older apparatus may be equipped with a manual traction control switch. If that is the case, consult the owner's manual.)

Antilock braking systems are now mandated on all vehicles, on all wheels, if such a system is available from the chassis manufacturer, as per National Fire Protection Association (NFPA) Standard 1901 (1997 edition). Antilock brakes, like the ATC, are automatic and not activated by the driver.

The ABS works using digital technology in an onboard computer that monitors each wheel and controls the air pressure to the brakes, maintaining optimal braking ability. At each wheel in each axle, a sensing device monitors the wheel speed. The wheel speed is converted into an electronic signal that is sent to the onboard computer. When the apparatus operator begins to brake and the wheel begins to lock up, the sensing device sends a signal to the computer that the wheel is not turning. The computer then analyzes this signal against the other wheels to determine if the tire should be turning. If the tire should be turning, a signal is sent to the air modulation valve on that wheel, reducing the air brake pressure and allowing the wheel to turn. Once the wheel turns, it is braked again. The computer makes these decisions many times per second and commands the air modulation valves to reduce, increase, or hold the air brake pressure in each wheel.

These decisions are based on the status of each wheel. But why is it so important to keep the wheels turning? The braking process is based on friction between the tires and the pavement. The physics of braking indicate that when applying the brakes to stop the apparatus, the operator can achieve the maximum braking force as long as the wheels are still turning. If the wheels lock up, most of the braking force is lost and the apparatus operator will lose steering control. The installation of an antilock braking system will prevent wheel lockup in an emergency braking situation, resulting in shorter stopping distances and the apparatus operator will be able to maintain steering control.

When an ABS-equipped apparatus is started, the ABS warning light will stay on for a short period of time. If that light remains lit or comes on while driving, there is a problem with the system that must be fixed. Generally, when a system failure occurs, the affected wheel and the diagonal wheel will return to normal braking function while the remaining wheels will operate with the ABS. (Warning: It is not advisable to pump the brake pedal in the vehicle equipped with air brakes. Instead, keep steady pressure on the pedal and modulate intensity as required for safe deceleration.)

One advance achieved by using the computer is the ability to interface the ABS, ATC, and auxiliary braking systems. What does that mean?

With the introduction of computers, antilock brakes are now compatible with auxiliary braking devices. In the event of a wheel lockup, the auxiliary braking system is automatically within milliseconds, shut off by the ABS computer. When the wheel sensors detect the wheel is no longer locked up, it sends a signal to the ABS computer, which in turn restores the auxiliary braking system. The ATC is interfaced in the same manner using this new digital technology.

At a recent trade show, I asked a representative of an auxiliary brake manufacturer why there is an on-switch for the auxiliary brake when its function is controlled automatically by the onboard computer. His reply was because the fire department wanted it that way. That's not a very good reason, considering most fire departments have limited knowledge of their systems. Perhaps the NFPA 1901 apparatus committee could take a look at this issue and eliminate driver controls for auxiliary braking systems.

This is just an overview of these systems. If your department has questions about a piece apparatus or equipment, consult the owner's manual or contact the manufacturer.

I'd like to thank all the manufacturers that contributed material to this column.